Max and Helen

Simon Wiesenthal is one of those extraordinary figures: along with his wife, a survivor of concentration and forced-labour camps, he is founder and head of the Jewish Documentation Centre in Vienna where he has helped to ferret out nearly a thousand Nazi war criminals – among them Adolf Eichmann, the administrator of the slaughter of the Jews.

He is often asked to explain his motives for becoming a Nazi-hunter. According to Clyde Farnsworth writing in *The New York Times Magazine*, Wiesenthal once spent the Sabbath at the home of a former Mauthausen inmate, now a well-to-do jewellery manufacturer. After dinner his host said, 'Simon, if you had gone back to building houses, you'd be a millionaire. Why didn't you?'

'You're a religious man,' replied Wiesenthal, 'you believe in God and life after death. I also believe when we come to the other world and meet the millions of Jews who died in the camps and they ask us, "What have you done?" there will be many answers. You will say, "I became a jeweller." Another will say, "I smuggled coffee and American cigarettes." Another will say, "I built houses." But I will say, "I didn't forget you."'

By the same author

I Hunted Eichmann
The Murderers Among Us
Sails of Hope: The Secret Mission of Christopher Columb
The Sunflower: With a Symposium
The Case of Krystyna Jaworska

SIMON WIESENTHAL

Max and Helen

Translated by Catherine Hutter

GRANADA
London Toronto Sydney New York

Published in paperback by Granada Publishing Limited in 1983

ISBN 0 586 05723 4

First published in Great Britain by
Granada Publishing 1982
Copyright © Opera Mundi 1981
English translation Copyright © William Morrow and Company.
Inc. 1982

Granada Publishing Limited
Frogmore, St Albans, Herts AL2 2NF
and
36 Golden Square, London W1R 4AH
515 Madison Avenue, New York, NY 10022, USA
117 York Street, Sydney, NSW 2000, Australia
60 International Blvd, Rexdale, Ontario, R9W 6J2, Canada
61 Beach Road, Auckland, New Zealand

Printed and bound in Great Britain by
Cox & Wyman Ltd, Reading
Set in Monotype Baskerville

Granada ®
Granada Publishing ®

This is a true story. The names of some people and places have been changed to protect the living.

Max and Helen

Prologue

I was on the train to Frankfurt. Since leaving
Salzburg, I had been alone in my compartment;
only the conductor, who checked my ticket shortly
after we left Vienna, looked in on me now and then.
I remained alone until we reached Munich, where
somebody asked me politely if the seat opposite mine
was free. I nodded, and he slid his small, elegant
leather suitcase through the half-open door, then
entered himself. He was blond, about forty,
impeccably dressed and was aware of the impression
he was making. He hung his overcoat carefully on
the hook beside the window, put his suitcase on the
rack, and took a good look at where he was about to
sit, then he wiped the leather seat with a tissue.
Now, at last, he could settle down, obviously
satisfied with all his precautions. He straightened his
tie; after that he took a good, long look at me, as if to
make sure that I posed no threat to the order he had
established. But that wasn't all. I could tell. He was
thinking he knew me and was racking his brains to
remember whether he should respond to me with
friendliness or hostility. He decided to be cautious
and hoped that I would help him to fill this gap in his
memory.

Since large numbers of people have seen me on television, the man's reaction to me was nothing new. Should I help him out? Why? Right now I didn't feel like talking, so I read my paper. I scanned the headlines. The date (the year was 1961) for President Kennedy's meeting with Khrushchev had been set. In a few weeks, on June third or fourth, they would meet. The man opposite me was still staring at me with curiosity. This annoyed me, and I found it difficult to concentrate on what I was reading, so I stopped. The man seemed to have been waiting for me to do just that. He started the conversation.

'Don't we know each other?'

'I don't think so.'

'Well, I'm not sure that we've met personally, but you look so familiar.'

'That's possible,' I said casually. I was not interested in making the conversation easier for him.

'Now I know! I've seen you on television!'

'Could be.'

'You've been on television quite a few times, once not so long ago. Am I right?'

'Yes.'

'What's your name, if you don't mind my asking? I can't think of it for the moment.'

'Simon Wiesenthal.'

He seemed pleased, or at any rate pretended to be, and since he was polite – he gave the impression of a travelling salesman – he stood up, bowed, and introduced himself with military brevity: 'Weber, Hans. I remember! You are the Wiesenthal who hunts down Nazis.'

I would have liked to know what he was thinking. When he had begun to realize who I was, his face had remained impassive, and that is an unusual reaction. When people who know what I do meet me for the first time they are usually hard put to it to hide their hostility or sympathy. But this man seemed indifferent. That was why I brought up the subject of my work. I asked him what he thought of it. I asked, 'In your opinion, are there any Nazis who have committed crimes?'

He answered seriously, ignoring the provocation in my question, 'I am sure there are. But others committed crimes too.'

Again someone who draws comfort from the stories of Soviet atrocities, I thought. It is always the same. Certain people in Germany like to use the excuse that the Nazi atrocities were not the only ones. They try to tally the crimes in order to feel less guilty. I couldn't help thinking that Herr Weber shared this viewpoint.

'What crimes on the other side do you mean?'

The answer was prompt. 'I was thinking of the bombing of Dresden. That was wanton destruction, don't you think?'

'I agree. If I had to list the war crimes of all participants, I would certainly include Dresden. However, I can't compare Dresden with Auschwitz

– but with Warsaw, Rotterdam, Coventry.'

I noticed that he was ill at ease. I was making him feel unsure. I seemed to have broken through his reserve, which was exactly what I had intended.

'Herr Wiesenthal, you are looking at me as if you would like to hold me personally responsible for what happened. I can't reproach myself for anything. I was a soldier on the eastern front. I obeyed orders like everyone else.'

What was I to reply? Finally I said, 'I only looked at you so intently because I would like to know what goes on in the mind of a German when crimes were committed and justified in his name.'

At this point he would have liked to have left the compartment, but that wouldn't have done for a man of such outmoded breeding. I was sure he would have liked to borrow my paper. That would have been a tactful interruption of our conversation. I helped him. 'Would you like to read my paper?'

He seemed relieved. Gratefully he hid behind it as I had done a while ago. Later he took a book out of his pocket. I couldn't read the title. It didn't seem to be of interest to him because he frequently skipped a few pages. Couldn't he forget our conversation? I felt his unease almost physically.

While he sat there looking miserable, the train passed through a large city, Karlsruhe: factories, chimneys, people hurrying to work, hurrying home. The man sitting opposite me looked out of the window as if he were searching for something. I gained the impression that he wanted to draw my attention to something specific.

'I wonder if we've already passed it. I don't think so. You see, I take this train regularly, so I know practically every tree. Oh no, no – we're just getting there. You see that factory?' He pointed, almost excitedly, to a big building not far from the tracks. 'Do you know that factory?' he asked.

'No. I know very few firms in Germany. Why should I know this one? It looks pretty large.'

'It is. They employ eight hundred men. The people at the top – they're the ones you should have a look at.'

I was puzzled. 'What do you mean? Do you know anything positive? Are you referring to one or more than one person?'

He hesitated. Perhaps he regretted having given me even this small hint. 'There are black sheep everywhere, not only in Germany.'

Cautiously I replied, 'No nation is all good or bad.'

The words seemed to calm him. 'In the factory I just pointed out, you could find a man, a little younger than me. You should look into him. He's just up your street. But please understand. I am *not* a witness! It's only something I've heard while talking to soldiers at the front.'

'Yes, yes. I understand. What's the man's name?'

'I don't know. And if I knew, I wouldn't betray

him. I am not an informer.'

'Who, in your opinion, is an informer?' I asked. 'You don't want to be paid for your information, do you? Whether this man is guilty or not, we certainly can't decide that here. But since there is a possibility that he *may* be guilty, aren't you in a way obligated to help us find out? Loyalty ends where crime is concerned. Isn't it also a matter of conscience for you? Isn't a generation that protects criminals sowing the seeds for a new generation of criminals?'

He thought this over and I could see it was painful for him. He couldn't look me in the eye but stared out of the window. I saw his profile and noticed the swollen vein in his temple. 'I think he is one of the directors, and is related to the president of the firm.'

'I am grateful for the slightest hint you can give me. I can only hope that there are not half a dozen directors who are relatives of the president.'

'I don't think you have to worry about that. As far as I know, the man I'm referring to is second in command.'

He changed the subject, telling me about his business and that he was on his way to Darmstadt. He took a black leather cigarette case out of his pocket and offered me an unfiltered cigarette. Then he rummaged in his trouser pockets for his lighter. He was trying to gain time. But I felt this was not the moment to let him go. Not yet.

'If you don't want to give me his name, won't you at least tell me a little more about the crimes he is supposed to have committed? When did they take place?'

Hans Weber hesitated again, then it burst from him: 'I was stationed in Tarnopol during the war, while the highway from Lemberg to Kiev was being built, in sections, but all at the same time. Along this stretch there were numerous camps in which the natives, probably Jews, were interned. These Jews worked on the road. The man I spoke about may have been the commander of one of these small camps.'

'That helps quite a bit. Thank you.'

It occurred to me that in the Lemberg concentration camp I had seen quite a few people who had spent time in one of these small camps on DG 4, *Durchgangsstrasse* (or highway) 4. If I was not mistaken, they came from the Zloczow area. They had been ordered there from Lemberg, to build the road. They returned, if at all, totally exhausted, battered, broken, and half-starved. They were separated from us after the first roll call. When we got back to the camp at night, they were gone. We heard that they had been shot. Nobody knew why they had been brought back only to be shot. We also heard that conditions in these camps were appalling, and that most of the inmates succumbed after three or four months. Very few survived. Private companies in Germany and annexed Austria were building the highway between Kiev and Lemberg almost entirely with prisoners from these camps.

I realized I would get no more information out of Hans Weber. Whether what he told me would suffice for my purpose remained to be seen. He got up and prepared to leave the train just as methodically as he had settled down in it.

'Thank you for your assistance.'

'Goodbye, Herr Wiesenthal.'

'*Auf wiedersehen*, Herr Weber.'

After he left the train at Darmstadt, I jotted down the sparse information he had given me in a notebook I kept for these kinds of entries. Suddenly I saw the emaciated prisoners of DG 4 clearly. How immediate the past can be! But whom should I send to Karlsruhe? I could look into the Lemberg and Galicia data personally and check all the records that had anything to do with DG 4. Perhaps the public prosecutor who served on the Lemberg case would know more. I would ask him. Perhaps there was a list of the camp commanders, or at least a record of the camps along DG 4. I could scarcely hope to find survivors.

1

A study of the Lemberg and Galicia files revealed very little. A man I was looking for, *Hauptsturmführer* Friedrich Warzok, was in Zloczow for a while. I found DG 4 mentioned in his file. *Untersturmführer* Richard Rokita, who had been in Tarnopol for two years and was now in a German prison hospital, might have had something to do with the camps along DG 4, but I did not come across any witnesses who stated that they had been in a camp on DG 4. Pretty poor results! But I didn't give up hope. My colleague, Peter, would continue to look in all our files for any mention of the camps.

I called the state prosecutor. He promised to look in his thousand-page file on Lemberg and Galicia for mention of DG 4, but I didn't count on much help from that quarter. Maybe I would come across a helpful clue in the manuscript of Tadeusz Zaderecki, former professor of Judaica at Lemberg University. The seven-hundred-page manuscript of this Polish professor, who again and again had found his way – which was strictly forbidden – into the Lemberg ghetto in order to take notes of what the tortured Jews there had to tell, had proved to be an important

source for the Stuttgart-Galicia trial. Seventeen
accused had had to answer for murdering Jews.
Didn't Yad Vashem in Jerusalem have an index of
persons and places mentioned in the manuscript? I
contacted the state prosecutor again and found out
that according to witnesses, there was a provisional
list of the camps on DG 4. There were two witnesses
from Zloczow who knew something about the
camps. One of them lived in Israel, the other in the
United States. Both doubted that there were any
survivors.

Meir Katz wrote to me from Israel, giving me the
names of the most notorious camps on DG 4:
Zalesie, Maksymowka, Ostrowo. They were named
after the small villages along the highway. We found
out from him that these camps consisted of a few
barracks and were surrounded by barbed wire. They
were situated close to the road and were guarded by
Ukrainian police. The camp commanders were
German.

Thus I collected information from various sources.
By now I knew that the DG 4 camps in Galicia were
under the jurisdiction of the forced-labour camps:
Lemberg-Jamowska, Zloczow, and Tarnopol. At
regular intervals, SS men came from these three
towns, sorted out prisoners who were no longer
capable of working, and took them away. What
happened to them must be clear to everyone. The
main camps were able to supply more replacements
than were needed.

We knew nothing about conditions on DG 4 in the Ukraine, the sector that led from the old Polish-Russian border to Kiev. But Herr Weber, our 'informer' from the train, had been stationed in Tarnopol. From this I concluded that the director of the German factory near Karlsruhe, for whom I was looking, was a former camp commander in Galicia.

Everyone who had heard anything at all about the camps on DG 4 was agreed on one point – the conditions were ghastly. If anyone escaped, the SS shot ten, sometimes fifteen Jews. This hadn't happened even at the main camps. The prisoners therefore watched each other constantly because the escape of any one of their comrades in misery endangered their own lives.

I had amassed information, but I had no precise description of the suspect. That was why I sent Peter to Karlsruhe with instructions to find out everything he could about the company. I had to know the names of all the directors. Two days later Peter called from Karlsruhe. He had been able to jot down the names from a directors' panel on the ground floor of their offices and from various individual doorplates. He had also found out who was second in command, actually two men. Their names were Werner Schulze and Josef Bauer.

'Please find out what you can about both of them. I want their personal data, where they come from, where they served during the war. The usual thing. You know what I mean.'

He knew.

'Simon, I can eavesdrop in the canteens. There are two – one for management, another for the employees.'

Somehow I didn't like Peter's idea. I was afraid he might attract attention and suspicion if, as an outsider, he showed too much interest in the firm's gossip. I had another idea. I told him to look up my friend, Fred, who lived in Karlsruhe. He would certainly be glad to help.

Fred was a German Jew. I knew him from the Grossrosen concentration camp in Silesia. He spoke German with a Saxon accent and came from Chemnitz, where his family owned a textile factory. They were assimilated Jews. Fred himself admitted that the only connection they had with Judaism was the family vault in the Jewish cemetery. In the camp Fred had agonized and cursed his fate. He couldn't understand why it should have happened to him of all people! He thought he had left his Judaism behind him. He was assimilated, to be sure, but not integrated, as he soon realized in Auschwitz. Was it clear to him at the time that there would be no point of return from this exile?

After the war he recognized me in a Munich restaurant and we became friends. Fred had a scar straight across his face, caused by the whip of an SS man. Fred's wife wanted him to have it removed with plastic surgery, but he refused, preferring to wear it as a mark of distinction. He told her that it would be a constant reminder whenever he looked in the mirror. Today Fred has a business in Karlsruhe. I can always count on his help, and when he decides to do something for us, he does it wholeheartedly, as if his own life depended on it.

Peter came back to Vienna and handed over the information he had gathered, some of it himself, some with Fred's help. The man we were looking for could be Werner Schulze, in charge of personnel and the son-in-law of the president. He was forty-four. Or it could be Josef Bauer, the sales manager, over sixty years old. Peter recalled that Herr Weber had told me the man we were looking for was about the same age as he was, which pretty much eliminated Josef Bauer.

About the head of personnel we knew the following: Werner Schulze was born in 1917 in Waldsee near Königsberg. He was a Roman Catholic, registered in Karlsruhe since 1952, and the father of two sons and one daughter. He drove a BMW and also had a company Mercedes at his disposal. He was very unpopular in the factory because he had a violent temper. The firm had been prosecuted by the labour department on his account. Schulze was described as being tyrannical and uncontrolled. In 1948 he had married the daughter of the factory owner. He had been a soldier on the eastern front. He was a member of several prestigious clubs and liked to invite guests to bowling parties in the basement of his villa. He turned down any kind of political activity offered him.

We had his address. Peter noted that he was picked up every morning by a chauffeur in the Mercedes and brought home again in the evening, and that it would not be difficult to take a picture of him in either the BMW or the Mercedes.

'Not bad, Peter! In fact, truly remarkable what you've managed to collect.'

'I couldn't have done it without Fred. We're going to get the photos from him. But I have something else for you. Publicity material.' We looked at it together. In one of the colour photos we saw a conventionally dressed man in the pose of a manager, who was apparently giving orders to several of his employees. He looked like a typically successful director. We noted his red-blond hair. The caption under the photograph read: 'The staff of our personnel department.'

'That must be Schulze,' said Peter. 'Fred had a look at the publicity material too. He hopes to be able to find an earlier picture of the man so that eventual witnesses can recognize Schulze from his photo.'

I took a long look at Werner Schulze. I wanted to memorize his features. On the comparatively small photo they were only vaguely recognizable. I had the picture enlarged and several prints made in order to be able to show them to witnesses. I knew it would be difficult to recognize someone from a photograph in which he was twenty years older than one remembered him. Still, it was worth the effort. With a striking face it would have been easy, but this was a face like dozens of others. Only the area around the mouth seemed especially sharply defined. As a factor of recognition, however, it would hardly suffice.

I phoned Fred and thanked him for his help. He told me that he would be in Vienna in two days' time for a business conference. We arranged to meet in the afternoon at my office.

Two days later at six p.m., Peter ushered Fred into my office. After we'd greeted each other Peter looked at us expectantly. I hated to disappoint him, but I had to ask him to leave us alone. It has always been my principle that none of my colleagues may know more about an incomplete case than is necessary for their collaboration.

After Peter had left, obviously hurt, I asked, 'Tell me, Fred, how did you get the data on Schulze?'

'Through a bank.'

'Through a bank?'

'Yes. I'm sure you know that all financial institutions have an information service. My bank once saved me from a disastrous business deal in the same way. I've known one of the vice-presidents for years. I told him that a certain Schulze, for reasons unknown to me, was anxious to leave his firm where he had been a director for years and that he wanted to be independent. I said he had made me a business offer, and I had to come to a decision in six days.

Since I was a Jew and had spent time in a concentration camp, I could only go into business with someone who had no criminal record during the Nazi period. Surely he could understand that. Four days later I had the material on Schulze. Here is the original data. Make notes, and then destroy it.'

I read the report: financial situation, a court order to pay damages for libel, a law suit, still unresolved, regarding the purchase of real estate, the testimony of neighbours revealing that he was not popular.

'Not a very likeable fellow. Were you able to get an old picture of him?'

'Not yet. My friend at police headquarters is on vacation.'

I thought it over. A picture of Schulze during the Nazi years would be best, although one taken during the immediate post-war period might serve just as well. I knew a police officer who was a member of the special German investigation committee for Nazi crimes. Right now he was in trouble with his superiors for being over-zealous. I phoned him at his office, and we agreed to meet at the German-Austrian border town of Freilassing. I hoped to get a photograph from some old identification papers. The officer promised to help. He had friends at the Karlsruhe headquarters who would look into the matter. I considered the fact that if Schulze had been in the SS or in any way a prominent party member, there would certainly be a file on him in the Berlin

Document Centre. These files were under the jurisdiction of the Pentagon in Washington, where ten
million members of the National Socialist Party and
their affiliated organizations, including the SS
membership list, were on file. However, the Centre
passed on information only to the courts, the police,
and a few scholars. Josef Wulf, historian and author
of several books on the Nazi era, and one of my
friends, had this privilege. I phoned him in Berlin,
gave him Schulze's data, and asked him to see what
he could find at the Berlin Document Centre.

Eight days later we received three pages of copy
from the archives with information on Schulze. We
learned that he had not been a party member, but,
after a time spent in the Hitler Youth movement,
had served in the Waffen SS, finally as an SS group
leader. He had received the eastern medal and the
decoration for the wounded. He had been an officer
in the security police in Zloczow. Before that he had
served in the middle sector of the eastern front, in
Zhitomir in the Ukraine, and had been wounded. So
it seemed there was nothing remarkable about his
army career. In the material there was a picture of
him taken in 1941. We also received something we
had hoped for: a passport photo of Werner Schulze,
taken directly after the war. The officer of the special
information committee enclosed it in a plain, not an
official, envelope. We compared it with the picture
from Karlsruhe.

There was a likeness, no doubt about it. This was

our man, in the old and the new photos. I called the state prosecutor, but he hadn't found out anything. None of the witnesses had mentioned a man called Schulze. Days went by. What did I know so far anyway? Only that a man called Werner Schulze allegedly committed crimes against Jews in World War II, according to a man I had met by chance on a train.

There were thousands of Schulzes in Germany and Austria, and plenty of them, I am sure, whose records weren't clean. But who was there to bear witness against them? Those who could have, approximately six million Jews and millions of other witnesses, died miserably – battered, starved, in gas chambers. Incriminating material, tons of it, had been hastily destroyed by the Nazi executioners at the end of the war. And still there was sufficient material, not available to the courts, lying around in archives somewhere in the world, unread, unused. Therefore, many cases remained unsolved. Was Schulze's case to be one of them?

I was not ready to give up. I recalled Dr Albert Glas, a lawyer from Cologne, who came from Zloczow. At the beginning of the German-Soviet war, he had fled to Russia and returned to Zloczow in 1945. As a former member of a Soviet investigation committee, he might have information useful to me. But Dr Glas didn't know very much either. I found out that many Jews from Zloczow were taken to a camp in Zalesie, a few also to Maksymowka. He had heard dreadful things about Zalesie, also that all the Jews there were murdered before the German retreat. Through his work with the Soviet investigation committee, Dr Glas remembered the testimony of several peasants in that area. Mass graves were also found.

The Zalesie camp was thirty miles from Zloczow. It was possible inhabitants of the town might still be alive, and they could provide information on the camp. To date nobody had questioned them. Dr Glas gave me the names and addresses of several people from Zloczow who had found a new home in Israel. He was in charge of their restitution claims from the German government. But I waited in vain for an answer to my plea for information.

At last – the turning point! Meir Katz had a visitor from America. His sister, Esther, came to see me, and I told her about my efforts to find survivors from the Zalesie camp, or from any of the other camps on DG 4. She knew of one, a doctor in Paris, recently arrived from Poland. I wanted to speak to him at once, so I tried to phone long distance. In vain. His name was not listed in the telephone book, which was astonishing. A doctor without a phone? I didn't know his address, so I had to ask my friend Leo in Paris to help me.

I had met Leo in the Mauthausen concentration camp. In 1945 after regaining my freedom, we had lost sight of each other and only met again ten years later in Paris, at an international historians'

convention. Leo also came from Poland and had lost
his entire family. He found the doctor for me in a
Paris hospital on the Left Bank, where he was
working in a laboratory. The doctor – let's call him
Max – really didn't have a phone, neither did he
have an apartment of his own, but he could be
reached through the woman from whom he rented a
room in the rue Amelot.

Leo went to see him there. He wrote that this
doctor knew about me and quite a few things about
my activities, but he didn't seem to like the idea that
I needed his help to bring a Nazi criminal to justice.

I wrote to Max. I enclosed a picture of Schulze
and related what I had found out meanwhile about
the Zalesie camp, whose commander must have
been Schulze. I begged Max to tell me everything he
knew about the man . . .

Three weeks passed with no answer.

When Max did not write back, I, as an experienced
Central European, took it for granted that the letter
was lost. So I sent a copy to Max, this time by
registered mail.

Ten days went by. Again no reply. Now I had to
ask Leo to step in again. The second meeting
between the two men was not pleasant. Leo wrote
about it, obviously annoyed. He had gone to the
clinic and waited for a long time until Max conde-
scended to appear. At first he had been extremely
reserved, but then he had explained it was impossible
for him to comply with my request. For certain very

personal reasons he could not bear witness against Schulze. In order to make his feelings clear, he would have to tell me the whole story. If Wiesenthal wanted to hear it he would tell it, but he could not possibly come to Germany or Austria. We would have to meet in Paris or Zürich.

'When he has heard my story,' he had told Leo, 'he will respect my position. I am so sure of this, that I am willing to abide by his decision whether he wants to pursue the case further, with me as a witness or not.'

After receiving the letter, I phoned Max at once at the clinic. We spoke Polish. Max came from Zloczow, and both of us had been to Polish schools. I wanted to know as much as possible, but his replies to my questions were terse. Yes, Schulze was commander of the Zalesie camp. Yes, he, Max, had been a prisoner in the camp. And that was all I could get out of him.

'Can we meet in Zürich?' I asked. 'I'll reserve rooms for us and let you know in good time.'

He agreed.

2

Exactly a week after this conversation I was waiting in a small hotel on a side street off Zürich's Bahnhof-strasse for Max to appear. The desk clerk called my room in the late afternoon and said there was somebody who wanted to speak to me. Max. We agreed to meet an hour later in my room.

Max was punctual. The sight of him shocked me – a gaunt, stooping man with sunken cheeks. His Adam's apple moved up and down. He was wearing a shabby grey suit with a black, wrinkled tie. He was obviously nervous. 'You must excuse me, please, Herr Wiesenthal, for not answering your letters. I shall try to explain why.'

'You don't have to excuse yourself, *Herr Doktor*, not now, since you seem to be willing to answer my questions. All I care about are the facts. But is it true that you are willing to let me decide whether you should bear witness or not? Leo wrote something to that effect.'

'Yes. That's right. With all I know about your work and about you, I leave the decision in your hands.'

'I am honoured, *Herr Doktor*. I assure you that you

are not the first witness who has refused to testify.
There are old, sick, broken people who shouldn't
and don't want to get upset, and then there are
others who wouldn't go back to Germany at any
price, or who have no faith in the German courts.
But then again there are those who feel that all Nazi
criminals should get the treatment Eichmann got.
The reasons given by witnesses who at first don't
want to testify are varied, yet I usually manage to
persuade them. I must say that many are grateful
afterwards because they know that to have refused
might have made them feel guilty for the rest of their
lives.'

As I was speaking, Max paced the room restlessly.
He seemed lost in thought, murmuring words I
couldn't understand. He fiddled with his tie, the
yellow stains on his long, thin fingers betraying the
fact that he rolled his own cigarettes. 'Did you say
anything?' I asked.

'Yes. I said that for me the war is not over.'

'To whom are you saying that? To me? Do you
know what I have taken upon myself since the end
of the war? You studied medicine and today you are
a doctor. I have an architect's diploma, but I don't
practise my profession. Instead I travel, seeking
criminals, trying to talk witnesses into doing their
duty as survivors and testifying against the men who
caused the deaths of so many people – human
beings who can no longer defend themselves. I
would gladly go to Zalesie. The trees and stones

would perhaps tell me more about the horror you were a mute witness to.'

'I do not consider myself a survivor, even though I am still alive.'

'The wounds we suffered will never heal,' I said, 'but we *have* survived, and the mere fact that we are still alive is an obligation. When I was freed from the concentration camp, I realized that there was no one for whom and with whom I could live. That was when I decided to dedicate my life to the dead. Six months later I found my wife. Still, I have remained true to my decision.'

'I understand you. Still, I can't . . . I dare not revive the past.'

'*Herr Doktor*, let us call each other by our first names. Try to imagine that I am Simon, a good old friend. Perhaps you will find it easier to speak.'

'Very well, Simon. I shall try. But I can't accept the word "old". Do you know how old I am? I was born in 1917.'

Max looked the same age as me although I am almost ten years older. His skin was lifeless, his hair grey and sparse, his eyes looked wearily into the distance. It was as if his surroundings did not interest him at all. His face was deeply furrowed; it twitched every now and then when he spoke. I could imagine the many long, sleepless nights that tormented him. He looked as most of us looked right after the war. What on earth did this man have in common with today's prosperity?

'Max, you look ill. If I had known, I would have come to see you in Paris. Why didn't you tell me? Or we could have postponed our talk.'

'I am not physically ill. I have a strong constitution. Otherwise how would I have survived it all? But my spirit is dead, Simon. I am finished, irrevocably. Perhaps it will help me if I tell you my story. Yes, actually I'm glad we've met, and that you want to hear what I have to say.'

There was a long silence. I did not want to press him. He had to find the courage within himself to begin.

'I told your friend in Paris that the decision would lie with you, Simon. Now that I am talking to you, I realize what a burden I'm imposing. I'm sorry to have to put you in such a difficult position, but you were the one who urged me on.'

'I see the purpose of my life in just such burdens, Max. I drag around with me not only the memory of what I experienced, but also the sufferings of all the witnesses who have told me their stories. Sometimes the borderlines get blurred, then I find it difficult to differentiate between what I and the other person experienced. Sometimes this identification is a handicap, on the other hand it makes it easier to conduct a confidential conversation with my inhibited partner, who needs my help.'

'Very well, Simon. You want to help me bear my burden. But how will it end? I will burden you without easing the load for myself.'

'In order to decide, Max, I have to know all about you. If you really want me to see your story with your eyes, and to understand it – you must confide in me absolutely. Without holding anything back.'

'I'll try, Simon.'

Max fetched a glass of water from the bathroom, drank, and started to speak in a leaden voice. 'I was born in the year 1917. My parents were . . .'

'Max!' I interrupted him. 'This is not an interrogation. I am your friend. Much of what you will tell me won't be new to me. I don't want a formal statement. All I want from you is the story of your life, your personal, private story.'

Max sat down and for the first time looked me in the eye. A great weariness passed like a veil across his deeply lined face. The rings around his eyes seemed to grow darker. In a way he appeared disappointed. 'But you want to know who I am.'

'Certainly. But the conventional tone in which you started off would have built an invisible barrier between us instead of helping us meet halfway. Still, forgive me for having interrupted you.'

'Very well, Simon. I'll try a different approach. I'll tell you whatever enters my head.' He paused, then went on. 'When I was young, I was an ardent Zionist. My father was a merchant and made just enough money to support myself, and my brothers and sisters. I dreamed of taking part in a *Hachsharah*, an agricultural Zionist re-education programme, so as to be able to emigrate to Palestine someday and

work in a kibbutz. That was my dream. But before
that I wanted to study medicine. My father couldn't
afford to give me a medical education, but he sent
me to high school and let me learn languages and
made great sacrifices so that I might be a doctor one
day. In Poland at the time, the *numerus clausus* for
Jews who wanted to study medicine was practically
numerus nullus. And then there was my love for
Helen.'

'Helen doesn't sound like a Jewish name.'

'But Helen was Jewish. She and I went to the co-
educational high school in Zloczow. There were
other Jewish girls in our class besides Helen, also
two Polish and two Ukrainian girls. But Helen was
the most beautiful of all, not only in her class but in
the whole area. I could watch her from where I was
sitting, and I never took my eyes off her, which
inevitably resulted in a rebuke from the teacher.
Actually her name was Helen *ja* Chavah, but her
best friends were Polish girls, and they called her
Helen. In time everybody called her Helen, a pretty
name that somehow suited her. Only her mother
and her sister, Miriam, went on calling her Chavah.

'She wasn't only beautiful, she was also clever
and sensitive. There was only one thing very wrong
with her as far as I was concerned – she was the
daughter of wealthy parents. Not that you'd ever
have known it. Many boys admired her, but she
soon gave me to understand that I was the only one
she was interested in. Naturally she was overjoyed to

know that I reciprocated her feelings, but I didn't want it to look as if I was after her dowry. I would have preferred it if she had been poor, like me.'

Max looked at me, and I noted his sceptical expression. He was wondering if I was seeing all this, undoubtedly the most precious memories of his past, as irrelevant. But then he sensed that this was not so. Obviously relieved, he went on talking.

'In those days, in a small town like Zloczow, a young man couldn't just start a friendship with a girl. Traditions were rigid. Without an official engagement, you couldn't do anything. I was glad, because it was my intention to marry Helen once I had finished my studies. We graduated from high school together. She didn't want to go on studying, and I was happy when she decided to stay at home with her parents and not move away to a big city.

'Helen's parents knew that I wanted to study medicine. Her father once spoke to me about it. I'm sure he meant well when he said that since it would certainly be difficult for my father to meet the cost involved, he would like to help financially. But my feelings were hurt, and for days I didn't go near their house. Then Helen came and cried as she told us that she had quarrelled with her father, reproaching him for being tactless. This led to a reconciliation. In the meantime I had been turned down by the universities of Lemberg and Warsaw, as had been expected, and had to look around for somewhere else to study.

'A relative of my mother's lived in Paris at the time. My mother wrote to this cousin because she found it perfectly natural for relatives to help each other. He answered at once and invited me to stay with him for the first few months. After that we could decide what to do. But this meant leaving Helen. At first both of us were miserable about it because we knew we belonged together, but I spent all my holidays at home, and soon we were perfectly happy again. I was a hard-working student because I wanted to complete all my examinations as quickly as possible in order to be with her. We wrote to each other almost every day, and since I had very little money, I had to save on food to pay the postage.

'After my third year of study, Helen's father suggested that we get married in July. It was 1939. But I was too proud at the time, and too stubborn, because I had made up my mind to marry Helen only when I could support her. I hesitated. Love and pride fought within me, and pride won. Our wedding was postponed, at my request. How often I have reproached myself since then. How much would have been spared us if I had let myself be influenced by my feelings at the time and not by small-town conventions. And it was this conventionality that ruined our lives. One word from me, and everything would have been different. I can't grasp even to this day that secondary decisions can have such catastrophic results.'

He covered his face with his hands, and there was

a silence between us. I didn't urge him to go on. Then, with a groan, he said, 'Why am I telling you all this? What concern is it of yours? Whom could it possibly interest?'

'Max . . . go on. Everything you are telling me is important and has meaning. It is a part of you, and the story of your life. And if you leave nothing out and hide none of your feelings, I may perhaps – I say perhaps – be in a position to make the decision.'

I recalled that Leo had referred to Max as a loner, a man who had reduced all contact with human beings to a minimum. This conversation was torture for him, naturally, but it also gave him an opportunity to relieve himself of his burden of silence. He had forgotten how to speak, but perhaps not irrevocably.

He went on.

'And then the blow fell. The war. Hitler divided Poland with the Russians. Our town went to the Soviets. I happened to be at home, on vacation, and was in Zloczow. To return to Paris, with or without Helen, was impossible. Helen's parents were in great trouble. They were rich. A Russian commissar and his family were quartered in their house. Helen's father ended up in prison. Whoever couldn't find work was deported to the "white bear" . . . to Siberia.

'Work was given to the local Communists. That was how the Soviets made decisions about life and death. Because everybody knew that deportation, with the hard labour involved, meant death. Unfor-

tunately, the Jewish Communists were the most
active. They wanted to prove to the new powers that
they were the ones to impose the new order on the
Jewish population. Zloczow, you see, was a poor,
small town with approximately twelve thousand
inhabitants, about half of them Jewish. A man was
considered rich if his family could eat meat three
times a week.

'These so-called wealthy people were to be moved
out. There were merchants and wholesalers among
them, professionals the Soviets despised because
they considered them parasites. Helen's family was
among these ''chosen ones'', but they were lucky.
By bribing one of the functionaries – even that privileged class was not above accepting bribes – they
and a few other families were assured that they
might stay in Zloczow.'

Max was silent again but this time, I was sure, not
because he doubted whether he should go on. Now
he wanted to be very precise about what he had to
tell.

'More and more Jewish families from the
German-occupied Polish territories came to the areas
occupied by the Soviets. They were fleeing from the
Nazis, but the Soviets sent them right back again.
Still, there were many who managed to stay behind
the demarcation line. They came from as far away as
a hundred and fifty kilometres from Zloczow, where
they found work and places to stay. They pretended
to be native Jews.

'Soon all the inhabitants of the province of Galicia became Soviet citizens and were offered passes. This was before the outbreak of hostilities between Germany and Russia. Many of the refugees and deportees refused to accept the passes, since they hoped the war would be over soon and they would be able to go home. Their refusal aroused the Soviets' distrust, especially of the refugees who could be suspected of spying.

'Numerous empty cattle trucks stood on the tracks of all stations in the so-called western Ukraine, a fact that worried a lot of us and led to the wildest rumours. Functionaries and members of the Communist Party in the area were summoned to the party secretary's office for secret conferences. Nobody ever found out what went on there, and there was great uncertainty, and in the end – fear.

'It was May 1940. Members of the Soviet secret police, the NKVD, were patrolling every town and village. Nobody knew who they were watching. One night they knocked with the butts of their rifles on the door of every house where refugees, or *byeschenyetz* as the Russians called them, were living. Those summoned were told to pack their belongings. They were going to be ''moved''. That night all the Jewish refugees from the German-Polish territories were herded into cattle trucks to be deported to Siberia. A cousin of mine from Krakow was among them. At the time, we were sorry for those who were deported. Later we envied them.

'Looking back at it all now, it would perhaps have been better if the Soviets had deported all of us. It would not have been easy to survive in Siberia, but at least we would have been spared the Nazi atrocities. Later I'll come to my suffering under the Russians . . .

'For twenty-one months we lived under Soviet occupation. Helen worked in a library, I in a hospital. Meanwhile Lemberg University had opened again, but I was not allowed to finish my studies there. I did not qualify as the son of a worker, nor could I study as the son of a merchant. So I remained in Zloczow.'

I knew what conditions in Galicia had been at the beginning of the war, and I wondered if I should interrupt Max and ask him to concentrate on the time of the German occupation. Until now a man called Schulze hadn't even been mentioned.

'I forgot that you come from that area,' said Max, 'and must know what conditions were like just as well as I do. Excuse me.'

Had he read my thoughts? But I was glad I hadn't interrupted him and felt a little guilty about my impatience. 'Please go on talking about Helen and yourself.'

'Yes. Well . . . we were forced to postpone our marriage, at least for a while. Helen lived with her parents in one room, but near us. They had permitted us to remain in our apartment, which lay in a poorer section of town. My elder brother married and moved out. My father could therefore suggest that Helen and her family move in with us. I can't remember why this didn't take place right away. Meanwhile, there were rumours of a new war.

'The Ukrainians seemed full of hope and impatience. They were feverishly awaiting events that they felt would change their lives decisively. On June the 22nd, 1941, we heard on the radio that war had broken out between Germany and Russia. The first German planes flew overhead, eastwards. The Russians were in a state of utter confusion.

'The young men of military age, especially we Jews, volunteered at once. At military headquarters we begged to be allowed to fight the Nazis. But they didn't want us. Soon the Germans were standing at the gates of Lemberg, and their arrival was eagerly anticipated by the Ukrainians. The Russians left in panic. Only trusted Communists, Jews included, were given permission to leave with the Soviets. Helen and I decided not to wait for the arrival of the Germans but to move on east. With very little luggage we reached the Zloczow town line, where we were stopped by Soviet soldiers. They had orders to let no one through. We would get in the way of troop movements. Anyway, there could be no question of retreat or flight – although every one of us was witness to the exact opposite!

'The Ukrainians grinned as they watched the Russians leave and papers being burned at the Soviet offices. They were happy and excited. Their leaders, who had fled from the Russians, had promised to raise an army to free them and to return under German protection. Now their hour seemed to have come.

'First the Ukrainians came to Zloczow in German uniforms, then the Germans. In their joy over the founding of their "republic", which they had been promised, the first thing the Ukrainians did was to organize a pogrom of the Jews, as they had done so often in the past. Many of their efforts for independence in the last four hundred years had begun with Jewish pogroms.

'Meanwhile, Helen's family was living with us. Both families hid in the cellar. Fortunately, an old school friend, who was now a member of the Ukrainian police, protected us. To have Helen near me was a joy in spite of all the misery around us.

'The Ukrainian units of the German army moved on to Tarnopol. Three days after their triumphant entry, their dream of an independent Ukraine was shattered. The Germans had different plans for them . . .'

I could remember this time, and how the Ukrainians had slaughtered the Jews. In Lemberg alone six thousand Jews were murdered within three days, during which time the Germans permitted the Ukrainians to do anything they liked. It was the same thing in Galicia. The Ukrainians took the male Jews from their apartments or picked them off the streets and beat them to death. The province, with Lemberg as its capital, came under the jurisdiction of Krakow. Ukrainian deputy policemen assisted the Germans, and were always especially zealous where Jews were concerned. That was their shabby substitute for Ukrainian independence!

'They certainly took their revenge on us, didn't they, Simon? Zloczow got a new mayor and a new town council consisting entirely of Ukrainian nationalists. The first decision of this new administration was to create a Jewish ghetto. It was to lie in the section of town where we lived, so we were able to stay in our apartment but had to take in two young people. The chief of police of Zloczow formed a Jewish council which was to deal with the Germans but not directly – for that the Germans were much too arrogant. Ukrainian police were to act as intermediaries. Then came the day when this edict was revoked. The SS and the SD came, the latter a security force. From then on we were "protected" by German police. News from Lemberg and other cities led us to fear the worst. Allegedly Jews were being picked up at random and were never seen again.

'I think it was July the 15th, 1941, when Jewish registration and a separate department for Jews seeking work were established. All Jews between the ages of twelve and sixty had to work. Those who couldn't produce a registration card, or had no job entered on their card, were taken away. At the time we had no idea where to.

'One day when we came home from work, the two youths who had been quartered with us had disappeared. They had spoken frequently about the partisans, so I hoped they had succeeded in joining one of these groups. Naturally they hadn't let us in on their plans. Perhaps they succeeded, perhaps they are still alive – who knows? Simon, I can see you are impatient to know something about Camp Zalesie and what I experienced there. I promise you – I'm getting to it!'

'How about ordering something to drink?' I asked. 'You sound quite hoarse, and frankly I could do with some refreshment myself. Let's see if the room service in this hotel functions.'

I was about to press the button to summon the waiter, but Max shook his head. Apparently he didn't want to interrupt his story; he didn't want to postpone what had to be told now. Instead, he went to the bathroom and came back with a glass of water. He drank it down fast, got another, and put it where he could reach it.

'Zalesie,' he continued, 'was originally a small German camp for Soviet war prisoners. Zalesie means something equivalent to "backwoods", and the place really was situated in the woods. The Germans had built the barracks for war prisoners a short distance outside the town. This was where the highway, planned to run between Lemberg and Kiev, would pass by. The highway was a military necessity because the narrow road through Tarnopol was not adequate for the German reinforcements to pass through into the central Ukraine and the southern front.

'At the end of 1941 very few Jews were employed on the road construction. The others lived as we did, in the ghetto, and were relegated to do forced labour in various factories. I was put to work in a place where old clothes and material were collected. The work was considered important for the war effort and could save one from being snapped up by the SS. So I got Helen work there too. All day long the two of us sorted out stinking rags, separated them according to the quality of the material, and packed those that were similar in large, round bales. We thought we and our families were safe until March 1942, when the SS herded all those who were not employed into cattle cars. Helen's family and mine were among them. Later we heard that they had been taken to Belzec and murdered there.

'New people came to live with those who had work. They told of resistance groups in the woods. So there *were* people who wanted to defend themselves, who were not prepared to wait apathetically until someone came, took them away, and murdered them. Exciting news! We called these groups, about which we knew so little, the Green Brigades. Although we had no weapons, we would have tried to get to them somehow, if it hadn't been for Helen's sister, Miriam, who as a child had contracted meningitis and had always been frail. To take her along on a dangerous journey would have killed her. Only bribery made it possible for her to get a pass for our so-called cloth-redemption centre. If she felt ill and couldn't work, we hid her behind the huge bales filled with rags, to protect her from being deported. Helen and I felt responsible for Miriam. To leave her behind was out of the question.

'In the meantime there had been more "action". Again people had been deported, destination unknown. It was perfectly clear to us that they were going to certain death. Another rumour added to our anxiety. The town administration had written, in the name of the Ukrainian citizens of Zloczow, to the governor of the province of Galicia, a brigade commander . . . I can't remember his name . . . and requested that the town of Zloczow be made *Judenfrei*, free of Jews. And we realized that we couldn't stay in Zloczow any longer.'

'Would you like to know the name of that brigade commander, Max?' I asked. 'It was Dr Gustav Otto Wächter, who was involved in the assassination of Chancellor Dollfuss. After the Germans took over, he became chief of police in Vienna, and after that governor of Galicia. After the war I followed the trail of this mass murderer. It led to the Vatican. But by then Wächter was dead. He lived in Rome under the name Otto Reinhart. He was given the last rites by Bishop Alois Hudal. At my suggestion, the public prosecutor in Stuttgart interrogated the bishop. When asked why he hadn't revealed Wächter's true

identity, he made all sorts of excuses. He was a
priest, he declared, not a policeman.'

Max stared at me, speechless. I consoled him with
something a rabbi had once said to me: 'God never
pays right away, but when he pays He does so with
interest.' This bishop would get his come-uppance
one of these days. I apologized for the interruption
and asked Max please to go on with his story.

'Well . . . I heard there were construction companies in Germany and annexed Austria who were
hiring labourers. Thanks to the intervention of a
former school friend at Ukrainian police headquarters, the labour bureau got us jobs with one
of these highway construction companies. Simon, I
don't know if you can understand this, but we were
happy, very happy, when we arrived at Camp
Zalesie, Helen, Miriam, and I. We looked upon it as
our new home.

'Trucks brought us to our barracks, which were
only a kilometre away from the alignment of the new
road. The foremen on the highway didn't spare us
the hardest labour. Their only duty was to see that
enough big stones from the nearby quarry reached
the construction site. Crouched on the ground, it
was our job to crush them. The foremen made sure
there were no pauses during which we might have
been able to catch our breath. There were to be no
interruptions. Those of us who had been detailed to
sift sand or to work on the concrete mixers were better
off. The mixers, by the way, had been captured by

the Germans from Soviet construction sites. This machinery had previously been owned by Jewish or Polish firms until the Soviets requisitioned them.

'There were a hundred and ninety Jewish labourers in Zalesie. In the morning we marched from the camp to the construction site, guarded by Ukrainian police. In the evening we marched back. We had a German camp commander, an elderly man called Heinrich Balke who, I imagine, came from the Todt organization.[1] Balke came from a village in Pomerania, not far from Stargard. He was glad to have been assigned this position and not to have to fight at the front. He protected us from assault by the Ukrainian police, with whom he didn't get along very well. He tolerated no excesses, all he did was to keep order. Somehow he managed to preserve a certain sense of justice.

'Simon, this man Balke was a blessing! We had been much worse off in the Zloczow ghetto. Conditions in the other camps couldn't be compared with those in Zalesie, they were so much worse. There was a rumour that Balke had been a Social Democrat and still was.

'Yes, Balke was decent. Under his jurisdiction there were none of the dreaded roll calls as there were elsewhere. If somebody was ill, they could stay in their barracks. Balke regularly inspected the food

---

[1] An organization founded by Fritz Todt (1938) for the supervision of all highway construction.

at the construction site, and reprimanded the foreman if it was insufficient. He never mentioned it,
but the way he behaved towards us was proof that
he found the position we were in unjust.

'I imagine his attitude didn't suit the construction
administrators, which must have been one of the
reasons why Balke was relieved of his post. The
official reason given was that the Ukrainian police
had complained about him to the commander in
Zloczow. The complaint was that he had
reprimanded one of their colleagues in the presence
of Jews because the officer had struck one of the
labourers unjustly, a fact the other officers disputed.
Balke said goodbye only to Martin Rosenfeld from
Bielitz, the spokesman for us Jews, and to his
mediator.'

'Is this man Rosenfeld still alive?' I asked Max.
'Forgive me, but when I hear a name I always ask at
once if the person survived and where he can be
found.'

'No. Rosenfeld is dead. He was the first victim of
the new camp commander, Schulze, the man you're
looking for. Balke warned Rosenfeld about Schulze.
He was a young SS *Gruppenführer*. He had been
wounded by partisans, was ambitious, a braggart,
and a great womanizer who had raped quite a few
Polish girls. We should be very cautious with him.
He, Balke, was worried about us; the least he could
do was warn us so that we would be aware of what
lay in store for us and, whenever possible, act

accordingly. He had heard this story in Tarnopol, and he felt it demonstrated what Werner Schulze was capable of.

'A priest in Tarnopol had complained to the governor that Schulze had shot at the holy pictures in his church. The priest also reported that Schulze, upon entering any house, looked around for holy pictures in order to tear them down from the walls and destroy them. Schulze was supposed to have told everybody who was willing to listen that the saints were nothing but camouflaged Jews. Later Schulze beat the priest almost to death. That was the only result of the complaint.

'The September day in 1942 when Balke was relieved of his command was a day of mourning for all of us, and his prophecies were to come true only too soon and would be surpassed. In no time Schulze turned the oasis of Zalesie into hell on earth.'

'Max,' I asked, 'do you know if Heinrich Balke is still alive? We should try to find him and thank him for everything he did for our people. Men like him deserve respect and recognition because, unfortunately, they were exceptions. Perhaps he is now the one who could use some help. After the war I helped many Germans who behaved decently during the Nazi period. They should know how grateful we are that they endangered their lives to help us.'

'Certainly. But I think . . . we . . . we can talk about it later.'

I didn't know why Max was suddenly hesitant.

He might have had good reason. If he didn't mention Balke again, I would have to bring it up and ask him what he had against my trying to find Balke. Now I didn't want to interrupt his train of thought.

'So . . . Balke was gone, and on the following morning we were chased out of our barracks by grinning Ukrainians. Roll call! We had to stand in five rows. A young SS man stood facing us, leaning on a cane. He began to shout: "Your idleness is over! Getting up and out for roll call will soon be a pleasant routine, and you'll march in an orderly fashion, not like pigs! Got it?!" Then he inspected the first row. "Dammit! And this is supposed to be a labour unit? I'll teach you how you're supposed to stand. In no time flat. I know you, you lousy traitors and swindlers. You'll get no pardon from me!" '

The language of the new supermen. Max had had to put up with it, and them, *ad nauseam*, and I too knew them well from the periods of my incarceration. We were nothing better than lice to them, pestilential insects to be crushed underfoot. But I have to take into consideration, what did these ardent Nazis know about us, about our history? Their outlook on life was formed in a parental home, a church, and a school, where Jews were depicted as the murderers of Jesus. That Jesus was a Jew was never mentioned. The Inquisition had already found that fact embarrassing, so embarrassing that it had tried to annihilate us, as if with our destruction that shameful fact could be dispelled. But it is impossible to explain rationally why in the twentieth century, with its pride in scientific achievement and enlightenment, a whole people should have been condemned as traitors and swindlers, and this view held by those who feel so superior because they are heirs of Schiller, Goethe, Bach, and Beethoven. I looked at Max. Could he guess what I was thinking?

He continued. 'With the new regime that came to Zalesie with Schulze there were also visible changes. A ''proper'' barbed-wire fence was put up around the camp and a watchtower was erected. Labourers became forced labourers. We were prisoners now, as if we were living in a concentration camp. Schulze didn't even trust the Ukrainian police. His camp was to be absolutely secure. There was to be no escape from it. A Polish family, who lived in a small house at the edge of the wood, was evicted, the house itself became part of the compound and Commander Schulze used it as a home and office.

'A few evenings after his arrival, we were confronted by a signboard, visible from quite a distance, which listed all the things that were now forbidden. Under Balke we had assembled in front of the camp entrance to start the one-kilometre walk to the construction site guarded by Ukrainian police. Now the day started with the roll call. Only after that could we go to the camp kitchen and fetch a mug filled with a warm liquid that was euphemistically called coffee. Then another roll call. We were counted by a Ukrainian. If there was a miscount, he started all over again, and we had to stand and wait. Martin Rosenfeld, who had formerly attended to all written work during the day, now had to do it in an hour before work and then move out with us. His wife, who had lived in one room with him, was moved to the women's barracks.

'The Ukrainians demanded that we Jews salute them however many times a day we saw them. Schulze initiated bed inspection. This was one of his specialities. The name of the prisoner was tacked over every bed, if you could call it that. The bed consisted of unplaned boards with a thin layer of straw on it, and over that a blanket. While we were at the construction site, Schulze inspected the barracks and wrote down the names of those who in his opinion had not made their beds neatly. In the evening Rosenfeld had to tell the wretched delinquents that they were to report to Schulze. They came back badly beaten. Fearfully a few people would get up ahead of time to make their beds so meticulously that not even Schulze could find anything wrong. The results were nil. However hard we tried, he could always find something that didn't suit him. Not a day passed without somebody being beaten up. For this purpose Schulze used the cane he had been leaning on the first day we had seen him. We found out from a Ukrainian, who was evidently not as ill-disposed to us as the others, that even when Schulze found everything in order, he would mess up a bed or two with his cane. This was to be proof of the slovenliness of his prisoners! In two weeks his notebook was full, and almost every one of us had fallen victim to this special treatment of his.

'We lived all day in fear of the evening. This fear naturally had a negative effect on our work. One day when the foreman complained that our performance was not satisfactory, Martin Rosenfeld was so incautious as to complain about the commander. The foreman called Schulze, and Rosenfeld's fate was sealed.'

'Max, I am going to order two glasses of vodka for us, or better still – a bottle. Or would you prefer to drink something else?'

'You are right, Simon. We could do with "a hundred per cent shot". Do you know the Russian expression? "You need half a litre to understand anything!" '

The waiter brought the vodka, Polish vodka of course, and ice cold. The look he gave us seemed to say that he didn't think much of guests who ordered drinks by the bottle. Max drank a glass, followed it fast with a second, noticed that I hadn't finished my first, and grinned. 'You don't seem to need alcohol to bear the dreadful truth, but I do. The schnapps is just right. What I have told you until now is nothing compared with what is yet to come. You asked for it. *Prosit*, my friend!'

I responded to his toast and braced myself for the fact that our conversation, which until now had certainly not been light, would become even more enervating as the emotional events were revealed. If only Max were not so easily excited.

'One day Schulze noticed that the head of one of the prisoners whom he had beaten was bandaged. "Who bandaged you?" he asked. The prisoner nodded in my direction. Schulze glared at me and asked, "Are you a doctor?" "No," I replied. "A student of medicine." "That's good enough for the goddamn Jews. As far as I'm concerned, you can look after someone who's broken a leg too. In return you are relieved of the stone crushing," he added, almost graciously.

'I am sure Schulze thought it was great that he now had a camp doctor. "I promise you," he said, "that you'll have plenty to do. The way you people work is scandalous. That's got to change, even if I have to beat you all day. The men at the front need that road, and they need it fast. And if it kills you all, so be it. The SS can send us plenty of replacements. We have plenty of Jews!"

'I see I've got completely away from Rosenfeld, but I want to tell you what happened to him after he complained. It was the day after Schulze had made me "camp doctor". That evening he was standing at the entrance to the camp when we came back. He made Rosenfeld step out of line; the rest of us were sent to our barracks. Schulze went to his private quarters with Rosenfeld. Half an hour later a Ukrainian came for me. I walked into Schulze's office and found Rosenfeld lying unconscious on the floor. With a gesture Schulze gave me to understand that I was to remove him. I couldn't carry him alone. Schulze sent for a second man, and we carried Rosenfeld to my corner of the barracks and poured water over him. It was all we could do. There was very little life left in him. He was bleeding internally. I realized that he couldn't be saved, but I wanted to ease his pain. However, Schulze saw to it that this too was impossible. He refused to hand out any medication.

'Next day we had to go to work as usual. I too had to go along, in spite of pleading desperately to stay. Rosenfeld remained behind, alone. When we came back in the evening, he was dead. The Ukrainians removed his body without letting his wife see it.

'All of us had loved and admired Rosenfeld, a courageous and kind man. He must have been around fifty. Helen tried to comfort his wife, as far as one could comfort anyone under those conditions.'

I could see tears in Max's eyes. He tried hard to control them. 'It was the first murder at the camp,' he said.

I thought, *Now I must calm him*. 'Since Rosenfeld didn't die right away, it was ''only'' manslaughter, according to German law, and the penalty for that expires in fifteen years as a crime committed during the war, counting from the founding of the *Bundes-republik* in 1949. Unless it can be proved that it was Schulze's intention to kill the prisoner. Max, exactly when did Schulze murder Rosenfeld?'

'In the middle of October 1943. Three weeks after he replaced Balke.'

While Max was talking, I tried surreptitiously to jot down the names Balke and Rosenfeld. Max saw me. 'And that's how life becomes a statistic,' he said, 'and blood becomes paper. One could go mad, Simon!'

'Max, do you really believe that I'd be sitting here with you now if I were concerned only with a statistical evaluation of crimes?'

Max gave me a sharp look, and I found the reproach in his eyes hard to bear. In order to distract him, I showed him the pictures of Schulze. He cast a glance at them from a distance. 'Yes, by God, that's him! The beast. His face is burned into my memory. I shall never forget it! I would recognize him any day, anywhere, if only by the way he moves. I could sense his nearness even if I didn't see him. And what's more, I saw his face not long ago. But that doesn't come in now. Not yet!'

He took a deep breath; he seemed unable to free himself of the memory. I began to wonder if he had forgotten me and what I wanted from him. At last, minutes later, he seemed to realize again why we were here, in a small, narrow hotel room, squashed between a bed and a wardrobe.

'Balke rarely visited the construction site, unlike Schulze, who came frequently. He would creep up on us from the side, across a field path. Suddenly there he was, in our midst. If a prisoner was sitting for a moment, not crushing stones, Schulze wrote down his name. When we got back to camp in the evening, the man would be ordered to report to Schulze, and got his beating. After Rosenfeld's death all of us knew what we could expect. Fortunately, Helen and Miriam were sifting sand or doing other, lighter work. Since Balke left, we couldn't meet in the evenings any more. Before that the women had been able to exchange an article of clothing for food, and cook for us. Schulze put a stop to all that immediately. ''What? Men and women together? Unbelievable! I'll have no pregnant women in my camp. I don't need any people who can't work around here!'' He ordered a Ukrainian to stand guard in front of the women's barracks day and night. Once he told me that to his disgust his suggestion that the camp be lit at night had been turned down by his superiors. He was furious.

'I had set up a sort of emergency space in a corner of our barracks. Since Schulze was anxious to make a good impression if there was ever an inspection of the camp, he didn't stop me. He wanted to prove his forthrightness by showing that he had a camp doctor and a sick bay of sorts. This alibi also had its good aspects for the inmates. One day I received from Schulze a quantity of bandages, some medication, and medical instruments, also for dental work. Schulze was expecting an inspection from the main camp in Lemberg. He therefore had us fix up a laundry so that he could present clean prisoners. He made us plant flowers in front of his house and all the barracks. A murderer who liked flowers . . . When the gentlemen arrived we had to march off to work singing. For days we practised doing this!

'At the roll calls Schulze read excerpts from Hitler's speeches. For those who couldn't understand German, one of the prisoners had to translate. Also Schulze's sarcastic commentary: what good fortune it was for us subhumans to be allowed to work on such a vast project which would lead to a new, clean, and better world! At the end he usually threatened that whoever tried to throw a spanner in the works would be sent off to where so many of the "swine Jews" had gone. One day when Schulze came back from Zloczow, he told me triumphantly that the town was now cleared of all its Jews. *Judenfrei*. He was obviously pleased not to be "bothered any more by the fearful eyes of the cowardly Jews".

'In Zalesie life became increasingly unbearable. The number of injured rose rapidly, many of the prisoners were too weak or ill to work, others simply collapsed during the roll call. It didn't take long for the SS to drive up with trucks to take away those unfit to work. Three days later thirty Jews arrived from Kamionki, a camp near Tarnopol. Among them was Gershon Halpern, an engineering student, who had made contact with a resistance group while in Kamionki. We became friends. We sat together on many evenings and discussed how we could escape from this hell.

'Schulze seemed to want to see just how far he could go with his fiendish game. He found torture fun. To this day I can still hear the screams of the tormented, especially those of a particular boy. He had tried to escape and been caught by a Ukrainian policeman about a hundred metres outside the camp. The officer handed the boy over to Schulze. When I heard him screaming with pain, I did something that was forbidden: I went over to Schulze's house. The boy was on his feet, leaning over the back of a chair. Schulze was beating him with his cane, aiming at the kidneys every time. ''What are you doing here?'' he yelled at me, his face scarlet.

'I implored him, ''Have mercy on the boy, *Herr Kommandant!* He's only a child!''

'Schulze laughed derisively, but he stopped beating the boy. Exhausted himself, he stood up straight; the boy slid to the ground, unconscious. ''Take this shit along with you and patch him up,'' Schulze cried. ''You Jews are such famous doctors. But no Jewish medicine can cure what I can do with my cane. You'll soon find that out!''

'I couldn't move. I was paralysed by rage and my own helplessness. Meanwhile, his fury seemed to have passed. Without paying any further attention to me, he walked over to the window and opened it. ''Get out!'' he roared suddenly. ''Out! I can't stand any stinking Jews in my room!''

'I dragged the unconscious boy into the ante-room. There I laid him across my shoulders and carried him to our barracks. He regained conscious-ness before I got there and began to scream again. I carried him as gently as I could to my little sick bay, laid him down, and with the help of some comrades, undressed him. I didn't have anything that could really help him. Shaken to the core of my being, I looked down at this wretched little body of human misery. Somebody brought a pail of water. I dipped a towel into it and laid it over the bruises. That was all I could do. To this day, after all these years, I can still hear Schulze's triumphant words. He was right – there was no cure against his cane.'

'What happened to the boy?'

'You want to know what happened to him? Exactly what happened to all the others who couldn't drag themselves to work in the morning and couldn't produce a note from Schulze that they were excused. When we left the barracks the following morning, the boy stayed behind alone. Even I, whom Schulze had elected to be camp doctor, wasn't allowed to stay with him. As we left he was still whimpering with pain; when we came back, he was gone . . .

'He was barely seventeen years old, blond, blue-eyed. He looked like a peasant boy. He spoke Polish and Ukrainian fluently and could easily have passed among non-Jews. He had no parents, no brothers or sisters, in short – no one for whom he had to feel responsible. He hadn't told any of us that he inten-

ded to escape. A good-natured peasant woman
might have taken him on as a farmhand. Quite a few
of us were able to save our lives like that. After the
war I found out from former prisoners how they had
managed to get by as farm help or by begging in the
streets, in spite of the fact that they knew they were
constantly in danger. It was so easy to recognize a
Jew. All the security police had to do if they thought
they had a suspect was to make him pull down his
pants to see if he had been circumcised. For years
these unfortunates could only wash themselves in
hiding, so that their Jewish origin would not be
exposed.'

'Max, can you recall – did Schulze ever shoot
anyone himself? Did you see it? That would be very
important for an eventual trial.'

'As far as I know, he never used his pistol at
Zalesie. It seemed to satisfy him simply to beat his
victims unconscious. They only died later as a
result. According to the law, therefore, he could only
be accused of manslaughter. But for the prisoners it
was infinitely worse to die after hours or days of
excruciating pain, which I could scarcely ease, than
to be shot. Schulze knew this. He was a sadist.
Screams and pleas for mercy intensified his pleasure.
If only I had killed him! There would have been a
possibility. Why didn't I do it?'

He looked out of the window as if he could see the
answer to his question on the bare courtyard wall. I
was silent. How should I behave in moments like

this? It is a situation I have found myself in frequently. Silence was a possibility. The right one? Max
turned and faced me again.

'Again and again I thought of killing him with a
weapon I understood. Often I lay awake and
imagined the scene in every detail. I would come from
behind and give him an injection of poison, and I
would say, ''This is your reward for what you did to
the boy, and to Rosenfeld and Mottel and Leo and all
the others.'' What would have happened afterwards
was just as clear. *Hauptsturmführer* Warzok would
come from Zloczow and there would be a court
martial. All the prisoners in the camp would have to
pay with their lives for Schulze's precious blood.
Today I know that hardly anyone would have
survived anyway, but in those days we still had illu-
sions. We Jews, we eternal optimists, believed in all
seriousness that survival was a possibility. Simon, tell
me, would it have been right of me at the time to kill
Schulze?'

Again I couldn't answer.

'You don't know either. If we had been a group of
conspirators who after Schulze's death could at least
have dared to escape to the woods to fight for our
survival, we might have had a chance. But we were a
very mixed group: men,women, young people, some
still almost children, and old people. Helen clung to
her sister, Miriam, for whom she felt responsible. No.
I didn't want to endanger Helen or any of the others.
This consideration for each other paralysed all of us

and stifled every thought of rebellion.'

'Max, you don't have to justify yourself, especially not to me. Many of those who survived reproach themselves just as you do. I don't know if you can recall the statements made during the Eichmann trial. Public prosecutor Hausner asked the witnesses over and over again why they did nothing to defend themselves. They described their situation very much as you have just described yours. To defend oneself meant to endanger the lives of others, and this they had felt they couldn't do. The question of resistance is extremely complex. It concerns not only Jews but other people as well. Concentration-camp inmates, whether they were Germans, Austrians, Jews, or members of other nationalities, had very little possibility of defending themselves.

'My friend Arthur Lauterbach, a jurist who was in a concentration camp with me, has spent years looking into the spirit, the souls of the condemned. He researched the history of criminology for cases in which convicted men who were innocent tried to offer resistance to their execution. He came across only one case: at the last moment a gypsy kicked his executioner. According to Lauterbach, the death sentence paralyses the convicted man, even the violent criminal. For Lauterbach the attitude of concentration-camp inmates was similar to that of those condemned to death who fear their inevitable finale without having the strength to protest. As an example he mentioned the Lemberg concentration camp in which we were incarcerated. Four thousand prisoners were guarded by at most forty or fifty heavily armed guards. Because the Germans, who Lauterbach feels had great psychological insight, counted on the fact that despair and the realization there was no way out would deter any thought of rebellion.

'Lauterbach's theory seemed to be confirmed in the Lemberg camp. The prisoners jostled each other to get their soup as if their lives depended on it. One day, when Wilhaus, the camp commander, shot into the crowd, those who survived went right on pressing forward for their soup after the dead had been removed, as if nothing had happened! Food meant life, so they fought for it with their dying strength. We were isolated and half-starved, and most of us spent the whole day thinking of our evening starvation rations. Crowded together in a narrow space, a better place on the bunks already meant a piece of life fought for and won. The day used up whatever remained of the prisoners' energy reserves. The thought of resisting the SS was infinitely far away for people who even stole from each other. And escape? Where to? Would the Poles, much less the Ukrainians, have helped us? Lauterbach was right. We had become helpless creatures, robbed of all human dignity.'

Max listened, occasionally nodding agreement, and it seemed that he was happy to listen for a change. So I went on talking about my conversation with my fellow inmate, Lauterbach.

'The German war of vengeance was not directed

only at the Jews, but against other nations too. But Lauterbach and I were agreed: the war against the Jews was easier to wage because the Nazis could depend on an anti-Semitism that had been deeply rooted for centuries. Poland is an especially startling example. Incited by agents, anti-Semitic propaganda found support in certain sections of the population, but there, where the Poles themselves were an oppressed minority – oppressed by the Ukrainians – there were people who had compassion for our fate, and on whose help certain Jews could count. Polish kings had brought the Jews into the country centuries ago to further and encourage trade, but they always remained aliens, even when they were willing to let themselves be baptized and to assimilate. Even before the Germans fell upon the land, radicals of the right and anti-Semitic Poles had prepared the occupation troops for the persecution of the Jews.

'In other European countries, those who offered active or passive resistance to the Nazis could count on the friendly support of their environment, but the Jews in Poland knew that they could expect very little help. Not only were we psychologically unable to resist, we also lacked all the strategic requirements. The people in the occupied lands who were not taking an active part in the struggle nearly always supported their resistance movements in every imaginable way. The Jews, on the other hand, were isolated from the rest of the population. They were surrounded by people who tried to take advantage of their misfortune and collaborated with the Nazis, and those who would have liked to help were either being persecuted themselves or too afraid to risk their lives.

'I have told you all this, Max, so that you might understand we Jews lacked all the prerequisites for a successful revolt. We stood alone, not only against the Nazis but also against the others. In order to be quite sure that their persecution would succeed, the Nazis went beyond their poisonous propaganda against us and threatened those who might have treated us humanely with the severest reprisals. Their lives would have been lost too.'

'I'm glad you think so, Simon. But have you any idea how hard it is for me even today in Paris to explain to those who ask: why didn't we defend ourselves? They simply can't put themselves in our position. That is why I avoid them. But I also avoid those who shared my fate and have survived because they too are always looking for an answer, and an explanation. What you have just told me, Simon, would make sense to them. Yes, that might be a possible answer.

'But let us talk about Werner Schulze again. He never got enough. There was a day when one of us disappeared from the construction site and was gone for two days. Not until then did Schulze report it. He reproached the Ukrainians for not watching us sufficiently. But that was all that happened for the moment. Then came Sunday, our free day. We were in our barracks, mending our clothes. A fellow prisoner, who knew how to do it, was showing us how to sole our shoes. Suddenly our barracks was surrounded by guards. A truck drew up. Two SS men got out. We had to assemble on the space between the barracks for a roll call. Schulze ran angrily back and forth, looking for relatives of the man who had escaped. Nobody stepped forward. "That is impossible!" he shouted angrily. "All Jews are related or have intermarried. There are married couples among you, and whole families! Don't you think I know that?"

'At last one of the inmates declared hesitantly that he was a cousin of the man they were looking for. Schulze told him to step forward; the Ukrainian guards were to bring him to his house. Then we were counted. The SS chose four men, told them to get into the truck, and drove off with them. Before the noise of the engine had died down, we could hear the screams in Schulze's house. Screams of pain and groans prevented us from sleeping all night. Next morning we were awakened an hour earlier than usual.'

Max was looking through me, as if he were not in a hotel room in a respectable Swiss city but still in his barracks, having to listen helplessly to screams in the night. His fingers were cramped in a tired fist. 'Simon, tell me where I can find Schulze. I'll go to wherever it is and kill him. I can't bear the thought that this swine is alive somewhere, quite possibly a respected citizen living in peace and well off.'

'I understand you, Max, but please calm down. Can you go on talking? The purpose of this conversation is to find out how and whether Schulze can be called to answer for what he has done.'

'Yes. So . . . next morning we stood as usual on the site between the barracks. Two Ukrainians dragged the broken body out of the guardhouse. Others brought a table and put a chair on it. A hook was fastened to the gabled wall of our barracks, and a Ukrainian attached a thick rope with a noose to it. Schulze ordered one of us, standing in the first row, to get onto the table together with the martyred man. "Put the noose around his neck!" Schulze yelled. The second prisoner hesitated. He looked as if he were about to faint. Then the martyred man helped him and said, "Don't sully yourself. I'll do it myself." As he said it, he laid the noose around his neck. The other man, utterly bewildered, stumbled off the table. At the same moment, the Ukrainians pulled the table away. The prisoner who had said he was a cousin of the man who had fled, perhaps only to prevent the vengeance of the SS falling upon too many of us, this brave man walked his last mile courageously. Not one of us dared to look at his dangling corpse.

'Schulze used the event as a splendid opportunity – that's what he called it – to give a speech. He assured us that we would never again see the four men whom the SS had taken away. If any of us should still harbour the foolish idea of escaping, five of us would be hanged in the efficient way just demonstrated. Five for one. He knew how to keep order in his camp without outside help. With which the roll call was ended, and we were allowed to proceed to work. When we got back in the evening, Schulze had still not removed the body. They say he photographed the unfortunate man. We saw one of the Ukrainians taking a picture. The body was removed three days later and buried somewhere. Nobody spoke about flight any more, since no one wanted to be responsible for the death of his comrades. That criminal's calculations had been proven right.

'Schulze's sadistic fury seemed to have been satisfied for a while, and he paid a little less attention to us. Then came the hard winter of 1942 to 1943. We found out from the Poles working on the construction site that the war in Russia was going badly for the Germans. It gave us courage. These scraps of information were a great consolation. When the frost came we thought that our work would be interrupted, but we were ordered out as usual, to loosen up the frozen ground. The construction company put up a shed with a small stove near the site. It gave forth a little warmth, and we were allowed to sit there when it was snowing outside, and crush and sort stone. That was how we were going to spend the winter. On days when there was no frost, we worked outside. Gershon Halpern, the engineer from Kamionki, said it was nonsense to work on the road in winter. In the spring or at the latest, summer, everything would have to be torn up again. But who believed that we were building for eternity? We certainly didn't!

'A month after Halpern's doubts about the

usefulness of our work, the Polish labourers were whispering that the Germans had suffered a terrible defeat at Stalingrad. They were radiant. Schulze's nervousness, and his more frequent outbursts of rage, seemed to confirm the truth of the rumour. He began to beat us up again and to watch us at work. Once he surprised one of us smoking in the shed. Schulze ordered the man to his quarters. After he had beaten him unconscious, he left the man lying outside my barracks, in freezing weather. When we got back in the evening, I found him there almost frozen to death.

'Meanwhile our situation had become practically unbearable, and there could be no thought of escape in the winter. The snow would have made it much too easy for the SS patrols to follow us. During the day, I helped in the shed, treating those who had been injured during work. It often happened that a man got a stone splinter in his eye or slammed a hammer on his finger. Actually I was kept busy most of the time, because the prisoners were unschooled and very weak, and had to work with inadequate tools. Whenever a foreman or a Ukrainian came to see what we were doing or Schulze took a look at us in the shed, everybody worked with furious intensity because no one wanted to be subjected to Schulze's special treatment. Then there were more accidents than ever.

'Helen and Miriam hurt themselves – Helen, luckily, had only a slight wound on her hand, but Miriam was worse off. She fell with a wheelbarrow, and the stones rained down over her feet. We carried her to the women's barracks under the sharp eyes of a guard, and I bandaged her as best I could. Fortunately, there were few disabled persons at the camp at the time. When there were many, Schulze simply transported them and replaced them with new, less used-up prisoners.

'You know these stories, Simon. Many of the witnesses with whom you have spoken since the end of the war must have described similar things. I am sure I am telling you nothing new, at best a variation on an ever-similar gruesome theme.'

'No, Max. There you're wrong. I don't deal with history in general but with individual fates. Every fate in itself is a building stone in my work, proof to me that I am right when I protest against the cover-up and the forgetting of Nazi crimes. Their stories must be told and heard. They should be written down and read, so that others, born later, can learn from it. Their suffering gives me the strength to do the right thing and may help others recognize that this barbarity, this Nazi tyranny, can never be repeated.'

My encouragement seemed to have helped Max. As he continued, he was calmer, more relaxed. 'Spring 1943 gave us new hope. Now and then we got hold of a Polish newspaper which the Germans issued. We read between the lines of the army reports. German victories were sparse. Expressions such as ''defence'' and ''a straightening out of the front'' became more and more frequent. In the evening four of us – Gershon Halpern and two other prisoners –

met in my sick bay, where I also slept, and discussed the situation. We planned our escape and began preparing for it.

'We needed blankets, knives, and above all a compass. But how do prisoners get hold of a compass? In the night the stars would show the way. Berek, who was escaping with us, had a watch. Gershon mapped out our plan. A sensitive point must be explained here, sensitive as far as I was concerned. I had to admit to the others that escape without Helen was inconceivable to me. I thought I could persuade her to come with us once the others had agreed to take her along. I was prepared for strong objections because to have a woman with us increased the risk. Besides, it was possible that the partisans whom we hoped to join would refuse to take us on because we had a woman with us. One thing was certain, we had heard it over and over again, the partisans rarely accepted men who were unarmed. But they needed doctors. That was our chance. All or none!

'I had to find an opportunity to speak to Helen alone. Under Balke this would have been no problem. Now all I could do was march to work beside her and speak to her in whispers. But there wasn't enough time for any mention of our escape plans. Besides, it would have been much too dangerous. Nor could we talk about it at work.

'I was able to persuade Gershon and the others more easily than I had expected when I told them that I could not consider escaping without Helen, especially since Schulze knew that we were engaged. (I never did find out who had told him that.) They realized too that to leave her behind would mean certain death. So we decided to get a man's outfit for her. I was to let her know the escape plan and the time.

'We spoke often about our strong family feelings, about the consideration we felt for women and children, the sick, and the aged. A Jewish freedom fighter would have wanted to take his whole family with him to the Green Brigade. But what fighter group could afford to accept that? Other resistance fighters didn't have this problem. They could leave their families behind without directly endangering them. We, on the other hand, knew that our disappearance was as good as a death sentence for our families. Since the idea of killing Jewish women, children, and the aged didn't seem to faze the Nazis, they made any form of resistance impossible for us from the start, for psychological and moral reasons. They had it all nicely figured out.

'One day I begged a Ukrainian guard who was on duty in front of the women's barracks to make it possible for me to meet Helen. I felt I could trust this man. He was always friendlier and more polite to me than most of the others, I imagine because he saw that Schulze treated me better than the other camp inmates. And that was true. Somehow or other, as the "camp doctor", I had a privileged position. The Ukrainian promised Helen that he would make it possible for her to meet me the next time he stood guard. And he actually kept his promise.

'But before I report on my conversation with Helen, there is something you must know which is of the greatest importance to my story. In the beginning Schulze had his house cleaned by a Ukrainian woman whom he had to pay out of his own pocket. Then he got the idea of getting the work done by Jewish girls. Naturally this didn't cost him anything. From time to time two would be detailed to work at his house. They were changed constantly because he was never satisfied. He would poke around every piece of furniture for any dust that might have been overlooked. If he found what he was looking for, there were curses and blows.

'One day – it was already spring 1943 – it was Helen's and another girl's turn. Working for Schulze was preferable to crushing stone, even if he was dissatisfied and bellowed at them. But, surprisingly, he seemed pleased with Helen and never shouted at her. Since he knew that we were engaged, he tried to provoke me by praising her appearance and diligence in my presence. He called Helen "a damned pretty girl", and regretted that such a beauty had to be Jewish. I kept my mouth shut and for both our sakes didn't let him rile me. When I was finally able, with the help of the Ukrainian, to tell Helen about our intention to escape, she was already working steadily for Schulze.

'In the little utility room, to which the Ukrainian guard had brought Helen, obviously frightened, we fell into each other's arms. It was the first time we had embraced since Schulze had come to Zalesie. Helen wept. Since I didn't know how much time the Ukrainian would allow us, I couldn't let her go on crying. I had to burst out with what was most important, instead of holding her in my arms quietly and caressing and calming her.

' "Helen, we've got to escape," I told her, and before she could protest I spoke with urgency about those who had been executed or transported elsewhere and been replaced by "new ones". One could easily figure out, I said, when the last member of our group would be "replaced". To stay meant a death sentence. Only the timing of the sentence was in doubt. Escape was the only alternative, a slim chance to save our lives. It was hard, but we had to face it. Those whom Schulze would hang in our place would die sooner or later anyway. All we would be responsible for was hastening their inevitable execution. I mentioned the war, which the Nazis were going to lose, no doubt about it. "But they'll kill all of us Jews before it comes to that because we have witnessed their abominable crimes. They will triumph over us even if they are defeated."

'Contrary to my expectations, Helen listened to me calmly, then the first thing she asked was, "Can Miriam come with us?" And I had to tell her that the presence of even one woman heightened the risk. Miriam, who was still ailing, would be too much of a burden and would endanger the whole effort. Besides, the hardships to be expected would be too much for her. And I confessed I had told Gershon and the others that if Helen wouldn't come with us I would not join them, and they had agreed only because they needed me, a doctor. I explained to her that the partisans considered doctors almost as important as weapons. She said, ''And how will Miriam get through all this without me? When they came for Mother I promised, I swore, that I would always look after her. I have to keep that promise, especially now that Mother is gone. I know that they will kill all of us here, you just said so yourself, but what holds good for me does not have to hold good for you. You, Max, have got to survive, and I am sure you will, so that afterwards, when it is all over, there will be at least one witness. God be with you!''

'Just as she said that, the Ukrainian knocked on the door. Helen looked at me, anguished. She wasn't sure that what she had had to say so quickly would suffice to make me go ahead with my plan to escape without her. We had to part. A parting forever? Neither of us dared express it. I took Helen in my arms again and held her close, as if I could give her and myself courage, then I pushed her out of the door and waited until the Ukrainian gave me a sign that the way back to the men's barracks was free. Simon, the memory of this conversation often eased my conscience later.

'That evening – it was already dark in our barracks, everybody was lying on their beds – a fellow prisoner, Kalman, who knew a lot about Jewish history, spoke to us for a long time. He had done this often, but this time – at any rate for me – his words seemed to tie in seamlessly with Helen's thoughts. He spoke about the Jewish martyrs of Trier, Worms, and Speyer, and of the victims of the Spanish Inquisition, whom we remember in our Yom Kippur prayer, *U-nesane Tokef.* He reminded us that in synagogue we put on the white robes of death to unite us symbolically with the martyrs of earlier days, while the women bewail their sorrow in their section. When Kalman stopped speaking, some other man began to sing the *Kol Nidre* softly. After a while all of us were singing, overwhelmed by the mourning ambience of Yom Kippur, and we wept.

'What were we so terribly afraid of? Those who had gone before had suffered similarly. Our fate was a repetition of theirs. That was what I thought of when Kalman spoke. Only our fate was perhaps even more difficult to bear because they had taken everything from us, including our identity as a people. We had no friends, no secure refuge, also no chance of financially buying protection and safety. All we had left was our lives, and to the Nazis our lives were worthless. ''We are not alone,'' Kalman assured us. ''All those who came and suffered before us are with us, if only we think of them. Not all of us will fall victim to the Nazis. Some will survive because Israel is eternal. As has happened so often in Jewish history, a few of us will defy our enemies.

Not I. Nor many of you. Our fate is the fulfilment of the prophet who said, 'A time will come when the living will envy the dead.' '' How often I have thought of this hour, and how truly Kalman spoke! I too envy the dead.'

Max was crying softly. How could I console him? I said gently, 'Max, please realize – Helen spoke the truth. You had to survive. You are a witness. Future generations need you because of the dead.'

'Wait and hear what I still have to tell you, Simon. Then we shall see if you still feel that I would be useful as a witness. Let's drink another schnapps. I could do with one now. Schnapps helps. I learned that in Russia. It made my long, hard years there bearable.'

'You were in Russia for a long time? I didn't know that. I'd like to talk to you about that too. But not now. Later, perhaps, or tomorrow. We should go and eat now. What do you think?'

'All right. If you say so. I'm not hungry. But perhaps both of us need a pause to unwind.'

3

In the hotel restaurant, where there were very few people at this hour, Max scarcely ate anything. The clinking of cutlery was the only sound that interrupted the silence at our table. To distract Max from his own fate I talked about cases in which I had tracked down the accused. I told him about the cowardice of those 'heroes' of yesterday who when on trial always swore that they had known nothing, and shifted the responsibility on SS men who they knew had died long ago. Not one of them showed remorse. All they regretted probably was that witnesses to their crimes, those who had escaped the murder machinery of the Third Reich, were still alive. Then I told him about those who have survived, the ones who give my persuasive powers a hard time, and with whom I have to be very patient because at first they don't want to tell me anything.

'I know, Simon. I'm a hard nut to crack too. I don't want to be troublesome. Why should I? But there are situations from which there is no escape. That's the situation I'm in. My hands are tied and there's nothing I can do about it. Nothing at all.'

'What do you mean, Max?'

'Wait and see. Soon you'll understand.'

'How much time do we have left anyway?'

'All of tomorrow. My plane doesn't leave until evening.'

To change the subject, I asked Max how he was making out in Paris. I wanted to know if he was satisfied with his work. Did he have friends? He gave me no details. Max wasn't the kind of man who wore his heart on his sleeve. His life in Paris seemed unimportant to him. He was withdrawn, a loner who had only the most necessary contact with people. That was why he chose to work in a laboratory and not as a general practitioner, who has to deal with patients. The past, which tortured him, crushed the present. Why this was so I would probably find out in the next twenty-four hours.

Whatever happened then would determine his life today. I could guess that much. But after what Max had told me until now, I must say I didn't understand why he refused to take the witness stand. He had given me such a good, comprehensive account so far, with many details which always enhance the credibility of a witness. Ideal testimony, which I would have welcomed as clear answers on other occasions.

He described everything so that one could see it clearly – the camp, Schulze, the Ukrainians – and had done so objectively in my opinion, only now and then overcome by emotional outbursts. Even if he refused to believe it, there was no doubt in my mind that I had found an excellent witness in him, who would be taken seriously in any court. Even a Werner Schulze would have to confess in the face of such convincing accusations. Was Max guilty of doing something wrong? Hard to believe. Was he covering up for someone? I had no leads. Helen seemed to have been of great importance to him. Perhaps she was the key to the secret cause for his agitation, his torment.

I was burning to know the answer to the riddle, but I had to hide my impatience. Max was exhausted, empty. He couldn't talk any more and shouldn't. I paid the bill and suggested that we meet again tomorrow for breakfast. Together we went up in the creaky elevator. His room was only a few doors away from mine. Max, who had drunk a lot and eaten scarcely anything, didn't walk unsteadily. His head remained clear. In his place I wouldn't have been capable of a coherent thought.

'You can hold your liquor like a Russian,' I told him admiringly. 'So sleep well. I'll come for you at about eight-thirty, for breakfast.'

'Good night, Simon.'

It was not a good night for either of us.

At three o'clock in the morning my bedside phone rang, long and shrill. Max. 'Simon. Are you asleep?'

'Not any more. You woke me. What's the matter?'

'I can't sleep. May I come to see you now? I've got to talk something over with you.'

Still drugged with sleep, I hesitated.

'Please let us go on talking. You may get an important call from Vienna tomorrow and have to go back. Then who knows when we will meet again?'

He seemed panic-stricken. In his excitement he had said *du* to me. Using the informal *du* myself, I tried to calm him.

'I'm sure I won't have to leave early tomorrow morning. You don't have to be afraid of that, Max. There is nothing more important to me at this moment than what you have to tell me, I assure you. But since both of us are awake now – very well – come.'

Less than a minute later there was a knock at my door. Max, in light pyjamas and a black robe, was standing in front of it. There was something ghostly about his appearance. The outlines of his figure merged into the darkness of the corridor, his chalk-white face stood out in the dark. I controlled myself with difficulty. I didn't know what to say. With a gesture I asked him to come in and sit down. Instead of sitting down in the comfortable armchair beside my bed, which I had indicated, he remained standing beside me in a state of great excitement. His eyes were glued to my face. With a trembling voice he said, 'I can't be responsible for what you demand of me!'

Was that the only reason he had come to my room, to tell me this?

I replied, irritated, 'What am I demanding of you except that you bear witness? I still don't understand your refusal to do so, Max. Until now you haven't given me a single valid motive.' Intuitively I added, 'Does your restraint have something to do with Helen?'

'Simon, perhaps I shouldn't trouble you . . .' He now used *sie*.

I interrupted him, told him that since we had started saying *du* to each other, we should let it stand, and I added that I didn't want to stop him from talking. There could be no thought of sleep any more. Max seemed to have been waiting for this invitation. Nothing could stop him now.

'In the end Helen's urging was decisive in my pursuing the plan to escape. In the meantime there were only three of us. The fourth man had bowed out. My main worry was how we could manage to escape without the other inmates having to suffer for it.

'I had an idea that was comparatively simple and might work. I would give Schulze a list of things that as camp doctor I absolutely had to have, and at the same time I would suggest that I go to Zloczow myself to get the medication and bandages. Gershon, who was highly respected in the building commission because he was the only one who had any technical experience, had to make a list of tools and materials he needed urgently. I wanted to persuade Schulze that we could attend to both matters in one trip. A Ukrainian police officer would accompany us, of course. And I knew who it would be. I thought of the Ukrainian who had made it possible for me to meet Helen. We intended to offer him money so that he would say later the SS had picked us up in Zloczow and taken us away in spite of our protests. It happened often that somewhere or other the SS urgently needed labourers and simply picked them off the street.

'My comrades approved of this plan. They found it acceptable, and it eased the conscience of every one of us. Yet I was tormented by doubt whether I had the right to leave Helen behind in this hell. One day, during the roll call, I gave her a sign that I had decided to stay. That same evening she was standing in my corner. I was startled, but she calmed me. She had lied to the Ukrainian and told him she had dreadful stomach cramps and had to see the doctor at once. Helen implored me: ''Max, you must go! I beg you in the name of our parents. Please escape. I demand that you go!'' I confessed that we already had a plan that would harm neither her nor the others. To be on the safe side I gave her a few pills and kissed her goodbye on the cheek. She left our barracks without looking back once.

'When she was gone, I threw myself on my bed, too exhausted to undress. There could be no thought of sleep. I was young. I wanted to live. I wanted to defend myself. The very thought of escape gave me the strength to go on. I wanted to reach the woods, the Green Brigade about which we had heard so much. I was prepared to fight and if necessary die fighting. I had no intention of permitting myself to be slaughtered like cattle. In the concentration camps the SS were the masters, but in the woods it was the partisans. I wanted Helen to be proud of me.

'At the first opportunity, Gershon talked to the construction foreman. He promised to give the man a gold watch if he could get passes from Schulze for him and Berek. Gershon cloaked his request with some important family business which he wanted to straighten out, and mentioned casually that he could bring tools and building material for the construction site from Zloczow. During the conversation, he let the man catch a glimpse of the gold watch. The foreman was won over.

'At the same time I reported to Schulze, who as in most cases was almost friendly to me. He once again praised Helen extravagantly and regretted that she was Jewish. Finally he asked me what I wanted. I gave him the list of medication and bandages, and explained how very urgently we needed both. ''I don't have the money for it,'' Schulze replied curtly. But I was prepared for this. I said that since most of the treatment was for accidents on the construction site, I felt that the building commission should be made to pay for the medical necessities. Schulze

graciously permitted me to bring the matter to the
attention of the construction manager. He wanted to
know what it would cost. On purpose I quoted a
very low sum. The man agreed but ordered me to
bring back receipts so that he could enter the
expense in his books. I took the manager's
permission to Schulze. So now nothing stood in the
way of my trip to Zloczow. When Schulze turned up
at the construction site that same day, the foreman
explained that he needed new building material
from Zloczow. He had two workers who knew their
way around there and he would like to send them.
Without my having to say a word, Schulze suggested
"the doctor" join the two men. He and the foreman
agreed that we should go to Zloczow on the following
day.

'This was lucky because we knew that our
Ukrainian was on duty that day. Since he came from
Zloczow, we expected he would be the one chosen by
Schulze to go with us. That evening I told the
Ukrainian what he should say when he came back to
Zalesie without us. I promised him a big reward.
Since he was obsessed by money, and liked me
besides, it looked as if our plan would succeed.

'Next morning the three of us were still present for
the roll call. It was my farewell to Helen. Would it
be forever? She was crying softly, inconspicuously. I
whispered to her in Yiddish, so the Ukrainian
policeman standing beside us couldn't understand,
that I would certainly come back to get her. She did

not look at me again. Neither of us really believed
what I had just said, but there was no way back now.

'A span of horses from the construction firm
brought us and the Ukrainian to Zloczow. First we
drove to the depot, handed over the foreman's list,
and loaded the material. Then the Ukrainian
ordered the driver to take us to the pharmacy, where
he let me get out alone. I gave what I had bought to
the Ukrainian. He shoved the medical supplies
under his seat, got out, and let Gershon and Berek
get out too. In a loud voice, so that the driver could
hear every word, he ordered us to go with him while
he did some private shopping for the commanding
officer, then he disappeared with us in the maze of
Zloczow's narrow streets. When we were sure we
were not being watched, we said goodbye to him. He
planned to tell the driver he had to wait for us
because the SS had taken his three Jews away for
some urgent work, with the promise that they would
bring them back soon. It was important to us that
the driver and the Ukrainian stay in Zloczow as long
as possible. It was the only way we could get a head
start. I only found out much later what happened in
Zloczow and Zalesie after we disappeared. You shall
hear that too. But first I shall tell you what happened
to the three of us.

'We left Zloczow as fast as we could and spent the
night in the nearby woods. We had only as much
food with us as was handed out for one day. Since we
didn't dare attract attention, we had no blankets

with us and no other belongings. Gershon had sewed a few gold coins into his trousers. I possessed nothing of value. I had given Helen the only piece of jewellery I had the last time I pressed her hand. Berek, whom I didn't know too well but who soon turned out to be very intelligent and determined, had hidden his treasures in his trouser belt. I had no idea what they were. Anyway, there was money in it because at first he financed everything we did.

'We felt confident. If everything went according to plan as we had envisioned it, Schulze would first wait for us to return, and then in a few days would report we were missing, that is if he believed what our Ukrainian told him. Then we could hope that the whole business would be forgotten.

'We spent the first night near the road to Tarnopol, only a few kilometres outside Zloczow. Gershon decided, with the help of his watch – for which the foreman would wait in vain – to proceed due north-east. That would bring us to Volhynia. Several groups of partisans were supposed to be there. We had heard of a Ukrainian group that was fighting the Germans and the Russians. Then there were supposed to be Russian parachutists who had formed a partisan group together with escaped Russian war prisoners. Who would accept us? We were young but unarmed, and could constitute a burden for a fighting group.

'We moved at night and during the day behaved as unobtrusively as possible. We hated to buy food from the peasants, but we had no choice. The peasants lived in fear. They were afraid the Germans might catch them doing something wrong. We had to reckon that as soon as we were gone, they would at once notify the nearest Ukrainian police station. Frequently, after our visit at a peasant's house, we could hear dogs barking, whistles, and shots. They were looking for us. So we soon restricted ourselves to farms that were situated close to the woods, so that we could run for cover quickly.

'Once we had to use force. Gershon had gone into a peasant hut, and we felt he was staying too long. We crept up to the place and saw that he was being held at bay by a youth and an old peasant with a pickaxe. They wanted to hand Gershon over to the Ukrainian police. They were probably hoping for the reward the Germans had posted for arresting Jews. When they saw us coming, they let Gershon go. We gave the young man a beating, whereupon the peasant woman brought us food. We pretended to be armed and ordered the old woman, her husband, and their son not to leave the house. If they didn't obey orders, we told them we would show them no mercy, which gave us an important head start.

'Simon, I spoke once to a psychologist in a clinic in Paris about the behaviour of these peasants whom we didn't want to rob. All we wanted was to buy something from them. He said the French resistance fighters had had similar experiences. The Germans were masters at intimidation. To disobey would have demanded a strong character, and strong characters were rare. To feed and assist partisans or fugitives was dangerous for the peasants, no denying it. Whoever got caught by the Nazis or was denounced could expect the worst. And all of them knew it.'

Now Max, the doctor, noticed our nocturnal talk was tiring me. He looked at his watch, excused himself, got off my bed hastily, and wanted to leave. I begged him to stay. He moved over into the easy chair, and I stretched out on the bed. He lit cigarettes for both of us.

'Max, please go on,' I said. 'Do you realize what it means to me to find out something about the life of the partisans? Authentic data? How our people defended themselves against their enemies? Moments when the hunted for once became the hunters?'

'Very well then . . . Our odyssey through the woods lasted six weeks. Since we only moved by night, Gershon's watch, which was supposed to function as a compass, didn't help us much, and we kept losing our orientation. We had no maps, and none of us was familiar with the region. But we were lucky. One morning we had just lain down to sleep when we were awakened by voices. Five men in civilian clothes were standing around us, talking loudly in Russian. I was relieved and happy to hear someone speaking Russian. ''We are escaped

Jews,'' I explained, feeling that this would make clear how desperately we needed help, whereupon one of the men, a broad-shouldered fellow with a machine pistol, said in a gruff voice, ''What? And you're still alive? They say the Germans killed all of you, but you're like vermin. There's no exterminating you!''

'A devastating reply. We were silent. Baffled. They searched us and found us unarmed. When we said it was our intention to fight the Germans, our mutual enemy, they jeered at us. Did we intend to go into battle with branches or stones, or scatter the enemy by roaring at them? I explained that I was a doctor and Gershon an engineer, and that in my opinion, even without arms, we could be of use to a partisan group. This seemed to get through to them. They ordered us not to move. Then, leaving one comrade behind, they went away, evidently to get orders from somewhere else as to what to do with us. At last they came back and took us to their camp. We had to strip, and they examined our clothing thoroughly. They found Gershon's and Berek's money. It was confiscated immediately, and we were told it would go into the communal till. They found nothing on me except a little photograph of Helen. ''Who is the *blatj*, the whore?'' I said it was a picture of my bride and meant a great deal to me. After a lot of talk, I was allowed to keep it.'

'Do you have a picture of Helen?' I asked Max.

'Yes. It's the one the partisan wanted to take away from me. Would you like to see it? I'll get it for you.'

He came back with something wrapped in tissue paper. He took the photograph out of a cellophane envelope and handed it to me gently. I was looking at an exceptionally pretty young girl, a Shulamith type. She looked like the Jewish beauties painted centuries ago: a noble face, a delicate complexion, and dark hair. The picture was yellow with age and looked as if it had been handled a great deal. I wondered how often Max had taken it out and looked at it.

'It was taken in 1938,' Max said. 'There were times when my life depended on this picture. It comforted me when I was in despair. It gave me courage when nothing seemed to have meaning any more. As you can see, I still carry it with me. During the time I spent with the partisans, it was like life-giving manna to me.

'There were about a hundred and twenty persons in our group, men and women. When I saw the women I reproached myself for having left Helen at the camp. Why hadn't I persuaded her to come with me? Among the Russians there were prisoners of war who had managed to flee, and a few Jews. We contacted the latter immediately and found out everything important we had to know about the group. They showed us on the map that we were almost five hundred kilometres away from our former camp! The partisans had radios and broadcasting equipment, and were therefore in constant touch with other resistance groups. Can you imagine how wild the three of us looked, how torn our clothes were, and what it meant after so many days in the woods to shave and to delouse ourselves?

'I wondered what the partisans would give me to do. I had no military training because the Poles, for the most part, had kept us from military duty since they didn't want to be bothered. We were category B. Still, the partisans gave us each a gun. I took part in every action and shot when I was told to. Our group was detailed to disrupt German transportation routes. Once we had to mine a train carrying ammunition. The Soviet information service notified us by radio when the train was to leave and told us where to lay the mines. We wanted to see for ourselves that the action was a success, so we hid some distance away. The train came on schedule, but the wily Germans had coupled two cars filled with sand in front of the locomotive. They were derailed when the mine exploded. The train stopped, and the German commandos shot into the woods. A little later, German planes bombed the area. We counted twenty dead and several wounded, and withdrew hurriedly without burying our dead. To add to our misfortune, we encountered a German patrol. Both sides fought bitterly. Not one of the Germans survived. I shot as if possessed. For me every enemy was Schulze, and it was Schulze I was killing. Berek fell. I was hit, but the bullet only grazed me. Gershon was more seriously wounded.

He had been hit several times. I carried him on my back until we felt we were safe. A Russian doctor bandaged his wounds after removing several splinters.

'We had strict orders to remain behind the German lines, but this wasn't easy because the line was moving west almost daily. Thus it happened that our patrol came in contact with a Soviet advance troop. As a result of a Russian pincer movement on the southern front, several German units were locked into a fairly large area, and we with them. Quite obviously we now had to disobey orders. We were in the Soviet-front area and therefore suspect. They moved our group about a hundred kilometres into the backlands. There we were interrogated by Soviet commissars. They wanted to know who we were, where we came from, and why we had joined the partisans. Orally and in writing! I asked to be allowed to join the Red Army, which people were permitted to do only if the Soviets felt they could be trusted absolutely. They assigned me to a military hospital in Rostov-on-Don, and that was where I happened to be when the war ended.

'All former Russian prisoners of war in our partisan group were taken behind the Soviet lines and questioned endlessly. Strangely enough, they were the ones whom the Soviets trusted least. They suspected their own countrymen of being spies for the Germans, with the mission to penetrate Soviet lines and be active for the Nazis.

'Before starting my duties in Rostov in the summer of 1944, I had read in a newspaper that a commission was being formed in Moscow to deal with war criminals. I read the news with great satisfaction, and at once wrote a detailed report about the SS murders in Zloczow, the conditions in Camp Zalesie, and listed the crimes committed by the commander, Schulze. I wanted the crimes on record, as evidence, which if the murderer was ever tried, could be decisive in reaching a just verdict. I waited daily to be summoned for a thorough questioning, but the Soviets evidently didn't want to know anything more. I was depressed and disappointed.

'Almost daily, before and after the end of the war, I met demoralized German war prisoners. In their misery they reminded me of the Jews in Camp Zalesie. So that's what was left of the former supermen! I couldn't hate them. I was burned out, empty. Somebody denounced me for giving a German war prisoner a piece of bread. He was an older man and reminded me of Balke, and I felt sorry for him. You know, Simon, a lot of strange things happened to me. All German soldiers were Schulzes to me, but in the prisoner of war I could see no one but Balke. The Soviet secret police questioned me for eight hours because of this anonymous denunciation. I was let go with a warning and was allowed to return to the hospital.

'But I had had enough. I didn't want to live in the

Soviet Union any more, and at the beginning of
1946 I wrote to the Polish embassy in Moscow,
asking to be repatriated. I think everything would
have turned out all right if I had known how to keep
my mouth shut, but I was in a constant state of
indignation, as for instance when I saw Jewish
officers being sneered at by their Russian comrades,
who laughed and said that they had probably bought
their medals in the bazaars of Tashkent. That's only
one example among many. I found these snide
remarks revolting because the Jewish soldiers who
had served in the Russian army were among their
bravest men. This was generally recognized. Many
of them had volunteered, still almost children, and
among them you could find the highest proportion of
wounded. This was one of my bitterest experiences.

'The war was scarcely over when the old
incompatibilities surfaced. A Jewish colonel with
many decorations, a wounded veteran, shot a man
in a Rostov restaurant because he had made fun of
his medals. It was the talk of the town. Shortly after
this happened, I was sitting in a harbour restaurant
with one of my colleagues from the hospital. We
talked about the case of the colonel, which had upset
us terribly. I was furious and said that Hitler was
dead but his spirit seemed to live on in Soviet
Russia. Next day two agents of the state security
commission came to the clinic and took me away.

'For weeks I sat in an overcrowded jail, with
twenty prisoners in a cell that would normally have

accommodated five. No one told me why I had been arrested. I wrote one appeal after the other to the warden. None was answered. I even wrote to Stalin, explaining my case and assuring him that I was innocent and had never intended to insult the Soviet powers, and that I was *not* a Fascist, since I had suffered enough under the Nazis. I mentioned that when I was with the partisans I had fought the occupation troops. The other prisoners, all Russians, laughed at me. Stalin would never get the letter, the letter wouldn't even leave the prison! Jokingly they tried to explain the power game that was going on: Soviet society consisted of three types of citizens – the first were in jail, the second had been in jail, and the third would be going to jail! "Every one of us gets his turn," they declared stoically. "So don't get excited. You're only going through what will happen to all of us."

'At last I was granted a hearing. But the examining magistrate turned out to be anti-Semitic too. He greeted me accordingly. "You can't depend on Jews," he said. "All of them are in cahoots with the enemy. I know you. I have condemned plenty of you. There you have paper, ink, and pen. Sit down and write a report of your anti-Soviet activities."

'He laid Helen's photograph in front of me. It had been taken from me when I went to jail. He smiled smugly and said, "This is supposed to be your bride, I've been told. Take a good look at her. If you want to see her again, write the truth." Then he left me alone. I hastily put Helen's picture in my pocket and wrote two sentences: "I have the Soviet Union to thank for the fact that I am still alive. I am innocent." The magistrate was furious when he read what I had written. He tore up the paper and yelled at me, "You made an anti-Soviet speech in a Soviet restaurant. I know it. I have witnesses. You worked for the Germans in a camp. That's sufficient. You are stupid. Only a confession could have helped you. Why didn't you beg the Soviet powers to forgive you? You'll regret what you've done, but by then it will be too late. Back to your cell!"

'Three days later I was sitting in a railway truck for transporting prisoners, like the ones the Tsarist minister of the interior, Stolypin, had outfitted for those banished to Siberia. The journey took a week. All the others sharing my fate had been condemned. I was the only one who had not stood trial. The guards allowed us to talk. This was exceptional. Everybody told his story and I told mine. I brought up the subject of anti-Semitism, of the indiscriminate condemnation of all things Jewish, of the shattered hopes of Jewish Soviet citizens who had believed in progress and that all superstition and the deep-rooted prejudices against the Jews would disappear. I spoke to deaf ears. The Russians were much too absorbed in their own fate to have any understanding of our problems. Only one of my fellow prisoners seemed to listen to me with sympathy. But did he really understand what I was talking about? I don't know.

'We arrived in Irkutsk. The city lies about two thousand kilometres from Rostov. A depressing prison. Again overcrowded cells, dirt, and stench. Very little to eat. What we got was unpalatable. The prison administration blamed these awful conditions on the war years, which made it difficult to get supplies. I became rebellious. When a guard passed by, I shouted, "Where is my verdict? All the others know why they are here, I don't. I have a right to a verdict. Tell your officers!"'

'One of the officers was a Jew. I tried to establish contact with him, at first without results. Not until they finally permitted us to get some fresh air in the prison courtyard, where we were allowed to walk in a circle for a few minutes, did I see a chance to approach him. I simply ran up to him. He yelled at me that it was forbidden to break ranks. All I could do was whisper to him quickly in Yiddish, "I am a Jew and you are a Jew. I am innocent. I must talk to you." He shouted at me again, and I went back to the other prisoners, crushed. But a few days later he sent for me and I was able to tell him my story. Shortly after that he informed me there was no data on me in Irkutsk, but he had written to Rostov for my file.'

How late it had become in the meantime, or rather – how early. I thought of all the sleep we had lost and looked surreptitiously at my watch. Max noticed it and was silent. I was afraid I had offended him and told him, 'What you report about your experiences in the Soviet Union corroborates what the few Jewish Soviet citizens who were allowed to emigrate had to say. Unfortunately, hardly anybody pays attention to such reports today, and I deplore this lack of publicity. Not long ago I spoke on German television about this Fascism on the left, as I call it. There was a public discussion afterwards. There were people, by no means Communists but Liberals and Socialists, who would have liked to stop me from going on when I declared that anti-Semitism in the East has its Fascist aspects. You should be telling your story to these people, Max. Perhaps they would take an eye-witness account more seriously than the opinions of someone like me. By the way, do you know the bitter Polish joke? ''You should be occupied by the Germans and liberated by the Russians!'' '

'It happened to me, this curse. But . . .'

He was silent.

'What were you going to say, Max?'

The strain of the last hours was noticeable. We were incapable of a serious conversation any more. I turned off the lamp beside my bed. It was almost light in the room. I said goodnight, a little abruptly. He left me without another word.

4

A few hours later we were having breakfast in the hotel opposite. Not a very pretty sight: two men after a sleepless night, one nervous, the other trying to control himself; two men who in scarcely twenty-four hours had become friends, two friends who could look back on a similar fate. I had a family, work that fulfilled me, I was needed. He believed his life was superfluous and meaningless. After breakfast we went to his room. The maid had been there to do the room; nobody would disturb us while Max finished his story.

'I think the last thing I told you was that the Jewish officer had asked for my file to be sent from Rostov. Just imagine – there was a verdict! Only they had forgotten to read it to me and have me sign it! According to paragraph fifty-eight of the penal code, I had been sentenced to five years of "reformatory camp" and five years' exile for anti-Soviet propaganda! The officer found the verdict mild. For what? For nothing! I signed it, and went back to my cell. My fellow prisoners wanted to comfort me. How? With an appropriate joke, naturally: "A new man comes to an overcrowded cell. The prisoners ask him: what did they give you? Fifteen years. What for? For nothing. That's impossible! For nothing you only get ten years! . . ." ' Max's smile was a grimace.

'We were taken to a labour camp, about a hundred kilometres away. I could probably thank the Jewish officer who found my punishment mild for the fact that I was assigned the job of medical orderly, and later as doctor. I didn't have to do any hard labour to earn the eight hundred grammes of bread a day we had coming to us. I suffered injustice and horrible cruelty in this camp, but I'll spare you the details.

'The *blatnoy*, the criminals, thieves, and murderers, were the masters. With the consent of the camp administration, they were given all the good positions. They got the best food and the best clothes. The political prisoners had to wait on them and were frequently beaten. And there were murders. And who do you think were the "political prisoners"? Russians returned from German concentration camps, former forced labourers, and prisoners of war. All of them had been given ten years only because they had been unwilling slaves for the Germans! In the women's camp there were two Jewish girls from Riga who had been freed by the Russians from the Stutthof concentration camp. They were so emaciated they could scarcely be expected to survive any more years of imprisonment.

'The life of a prisoner in a Soviet camp was worth just as little as in Zalesie. The political prisoners were completely at the mercy of the guards and commanders. The murderous climate, the hard work of lumbering, and the lack of food along with the wretched physical condition of the prisoners caused many to die a "natural death" in abject misery. "We don't have to beat you," one of the guards said. "You'll croak all by yourselves." And he was right. I spent five years in this hell. I was there almost until Stalin's death in 1953.

'Well, as you can see, I survived, always with the realization that my years of martyrdom were by no means over. I was "let go" into exile and had to spend five more years in Siberia as a *volnonayomni*, a word that comes from the years of slavery and means something equivalent to being "freely hired". I was assigned to a hospital in Irkutsk.

'The notices in the newspaper about trials against war criminals persuaded me to appeal again to the Soviet commission for Nazi war crimes. Again I sent off a report on conditions in Zalesie. I described Schulze's crimes in detail and praised Balke. They should find Schulze, but if Balke was in a prison camp, they should let him go. You see, there were still times when I was very naïve and acted impulsively. Of course, there was no answer, no reaction at all.'

'Max,' I said, 'you speak bitterly about German and Soviet camps. For you the liberators don't seem much better than the Nazis, and according to your experiences this may be true. Is that why you don't want to bear witness against the German criminals? Forgive me. Perhaps I shouldn't have put it like that, because one injustice doesn't balance the other.'

He protested. 'No, Simon. That's not it. I wasn't thinking in political terms. I have entirely private, personal reasons for my decision. But let me go on . . .

'So the five years of exile also passed. You can imagine how. But at last I was "a free man". The year was 1956. I could apply to the Polish embassy in Moscow for repatriation to my homeland. I was told that according to the authorities, I was now a Russian citizen, since I came from a sector of Poland which had been ceded to Russia. But Poles from this area could petition to be rehabilitated in what was now called "The People's Republic". However, Jews who, like me, declared they were Poles, needed a special permit. The embassy would write to Warsaw again. Meanwhile, I wrote to the *gorsoviet*, or magistrate, in Zloczow and asked if there were any survivors of Camp Zalesie. I included the data on Helen and her sister, Miriam – all of which I had kept – and also their former address. I received no reply.

'By now Khrushchev was in power and Stalin had been condemned. Rehabilitation committees were formed. One day I had to appear before such a commission. At last, in 1958, I too was rehabilitated. I received a piece of paper which stated that I was innocent, that the whole thing had been a mistake, and that my reputation was unblemished. A big seal made the simple truth official.

'But for many people the rehabilitation commission came too late. I feel ill whenever I think of it. Nobody mentioned them, and, what was worse, nothing was done about the people who had made the "mistakes". None of those who were responsible for these injustices was ever called to answer for them. There may have been a few demotions . . . who knows? But if so, no one heard about them. The Russian Schulzes were certainly never tried. Beria, the head of the security police, and his deputy, Abakumov, were shot not for their crimes but because they posed a danger to those in power at the time. The Russian people accepted all the terror as a natural catastrophe, or like an epidemic of the flu!

'I went to Moscow. I had a permit to travel and enough money for the trip. But I had no identification papers of any kind except for my certificate of dismissal from the Soviet camp and the confirmation of my rehabilitation. And bureaucrats don't like such meagre documentation!

'From the station I went straight to the Polish embassy. There I spoke to a very friendly, helpful young man who seemed to know exactly who I was. My numerous letters to the Polish representatives had evidently not passed unnoticed. Anyway, I got that impression. While I waited he phoned Warsaw, and I found out that they were working on my repatriation. I went back to Irkutsk feeling hopeful that I would soon have good news. However, three months were still to pass before I received my repatriation papers. I was assured that in a few days a transport of repatriates was going to be assembled, and this actually took place. In October 1958 I returned to Poland, a country that now called itself a People's Republic, a country about whose postwar development I knew nothing, yet I was to call it my home!

'I wrote to Jewish committees in Warsaw and Krakow, hoping to find out something about Helen, Miriam, relatives, and friends. The laconic answer was always: not registered. One of the Soviet commissions for Nazi crimes, from which I had asked for information on Camp Zalesie and the fate of the prisoners there, wrote and told me that according to witnesses, all prisoners had been killed before the Germans left the area. Feelings can be deceptive – I knew that – still I believed firmly, wanted to, had to! Helen and I *would* find each other again, even though all signs were against it. The search for survivors was not encouraging. I spoke to several people from Zloczow. All they knew was that the Germans had killed all the Jews in Zalesie before retreating. Others had heard of deportations back to Germany. The Jewish committee in Warsaw advised me to inquire at the International Red Cross

in Geneva. This organization would authorize the
Polish Red Cross to look for my fiancée. Some time
later I received the news that Helen's whereabouts
were unknown. She was not registered anywhere,
there was no telling whether she was perhaps living
in a foreign country or had been killed. Reluctantly,
yet of necessity, I began to realize that Helen might
not have survived the war. If she were still alive, she
would certainly also be looking for me, and her
name would have turned up in one of the files of
those seeking their loved ones.

'I received a copy of my school diplomas from
Paris, and from the Soviet Union, the confirmation
of my work as a doctor. I was able to finish my
medical studies at Warsaw University, after which I
worked in a hospital in that city. But I still craved
certainty over Helen's fate. Everything in me
protested against her death. But if she was dead, I
wanted proof. I found people from Tarnopol and
from Lemberg who had heard of Zalesie. Every one
of them repeated what I had already been told: there
were no survivors. For three days I sat in the Jewish
Historical Institute in Warsaw, looking through the
collected depositions of witnesses for any mention of
Zalesie. One witness stated that his brother had died
in the camp. I took down his name. His statement
had been made in 1946. It took me a long time to
find out where he lived. I went there and discovered
he had died two years earlier.

'In the summer of 1960 I was given a permit to

travel to Soviet Zloczow (Zolochev). The house in which we had lived was still standing. It had survived the war undamaged. I spoke to the strangers who lived in it now. I explained that I was looking for a young girl who had also lived here once. "Wasn't she with you? Didn't she ask after me?" A shake of the head was all the answer I got. I only realized later what a paradox my question had been. For me Helen was still the young girl I had left behind. That she had also grown older, was forty years old, was something I didn't want to think about.

'There were no Jews left in Zloczow who had been living there before the war, only those who had come with the Soviets. But a few Ukrainians I knew were still living in the town. They too corroborated the fact that the Nazis had killed all the Jews in the camp. There were no Poles left in Zloczow. The Ukrainians told me they had either fled from the Russians or opted for Poland. At Soviet police head-quarters, the militia, I asked for permission to visit Camp Zalesie. I explained that I had been a prisoner there and hoped to find out something from the peasants in the neighbourhood about the fates of those who had been incarcerated with me. The powers that be were conciliatory, and I was given permission. What would I find?

'The barracks had been burned; the charred remains had become overgrown long ago. A Ukrainian peasant told me that before the Germans retreated from the Russians, they had burned the camp to the ground. He and others declared that the Germans had taken the Jews with them. They didn't know where they had gone. I wanted to be quite sure, so I asked, ''They weren't shot right here?'' No. They could swear to that. A peasant woman remembered that the Jews had been taken away in trucks, she had seen it herself. Then according to her husband, four days later the Russians had arrived. I asked if there had been men and women whom the SS had taken away at the last minute. Yes. They were sure of that. So the journey had not been for nothing!

'Back to Warsaw, after brooding over it, I was finally able to remember the name of the Linz construction firm we had worked for. I found out that it still existed and wrote to the management. Perhaps a former foreman might remember Helen and Miriam and know something about their where-abouts. I did not receive an answer.'

'Max, why didn't you come to me? I am sure they would have answered.'

'At the time I knew hardly anything about you. I had heard your name mentioned frequently in connection with the uncovering of Nazi crimes, but that was all. I was terribly impatient and in a constant state of irritation and tension. I asked everyone I met about Zloczow and Zalesie. People spoke to me with compassion, as if I were ill. I didn't need their compassion. I couldn't rest until I knew what had happened to Helen, and if I got on everybody's nerves with my questions, it didn't bother me. It was the only way I could possibly reach my goal. And I was eventually able to prove that.

'Quite by chance, in a station restaurant in Krakow, I met a Polish woman who had been in the same high school class in Zloczow with Helen and me. Of course she remembered Helen, but she could tell me nothing about her. Stefa – that was her name – gave me the address of two other classmates: Wanda and Yadzia, who were living in Poznan now. They were married and had children. Stefa told me that she too had been searching for years. She was trying to find her father, a Polish officer, whom the Russians had dragged away. Since he was not on the list of officers shot by the Soviets in Katyn, she still hoped to find him. She had lost her brother in the Warsaw uprising.

'I had planned to stay a few days in Krakow and attend to various matters, but after my meeting with Stefa I decided to go on to Poznan because Wanda and Yadzia had been close friends of Helen's. I visited Wanda first. She didn't recognize me! No wonder, after all that I had experienced. I was tense with impatience and burst right out with "I am looking for Helen!" "Helen is alive," she said, just like that, and everything went black before my eyes. I had fainted. When I came to, Wanda was kneeling beside me, upset. She tried to make me drink a few

sips of water. It must have been quite a while before
I could finally stammer, "Where is she, Wanda?
I . . . I want to go to her at once. I've been looking
for her for twenty years!"

'Wanda gently explained that Helen had left
Poland long ago and was living under an assumed
name in West Germany, in the part called the
Bundesrepublik. The last time the two friends had seen
each other was twelve years ago. Wanda didn't
know why Helen had chosen to live in Germany, of
all places. Early in the fifties she had moved away
illegally with some Jews who were planning to
emigrate to Israel. Wanda showed me the postcard
Helen had sent her from Munich, and a Christmas
card postmarked Kassel. In each case the return
address was missing. But Helen had signed the cards
with the name she must have assumed at some time
or other. Wanda kept both cards in a small box with
other souvenirs, old pictures, and letters; she even
had some class pictures. Only one sentence was
written on Helen's card from Kassel: "Warmest
greetings. I have not forgotten you." Next day,
Yadzia couldn't tell me more than Wanda. Just the
same, I returned to Warsaw more hopeful than ever.
Helen was alive! I knew the name under which I
could find her. I imagined our reunion in the rosiest
colours. Now it was only a question of time!

'It was not going to be easy to get a permit to leave
Poland, but it was possible if you could show an
invitation from a foreign country. I wrote to the

registration bureau in Kassel, asking for Helen's address. There was no reply. Was Helen really living there? After all, it was only a conjecture on my part. Perhaps she had changed her name again. Anything was possible. Also perhaps the censor had confiscated my letter or her reply. Still, I was optimistic. No one and nothing was going to stop me from seeing Helen again.'

I wanted Max to stop for a while, and proposed we go for a boat ride on Lake Zürich, or at least take a walk along its shores. The sunshine looked inviting, but Max rejected the idea. However, he agreed to a change of setting. We walked for a while, then sat down on the terrace of a restaurant facing the lake. From here we had a magnificent view of the landscape. Here we could breathe better than in the narrow hotel room with its view of the gloomy courtyard. We had lunch. Had it been up to me, we would have sat on the terrace a while longer, but Max insisted we leave. 'I can't go on talking here, Simon. I'm sorry, but please let's go back to the hotel.' I found the narrowness of the hotel room oppressive, but it seemed to stimulate him.

'It never occurred to me that Helen might have married,' Max admitted. 'There was no room in my heart for such a consideration. I was possessed by one thought only: how could I get to Germany? There were men who would smuggle you across the border, for money, but I didn't have the money, and the risk seemed too great. There had to be a safer

way to reach Helen. I was advised to take a holiday
in Yugoslavia and flee to Austria from there.

'This seemed to make sense, so in the summer I
booked a trip to Yugoslavia. With a group of tourists
I travelled by bus through Czechoslovakia and
Hungary. The tour leader had our passports. We
were taken to an attractive hotel on the seashore,
beautiful surroundings, but they made no impression on me. All I was looking for was contact with
tourists from West Germany or Austria. I was
counting on their help. Cautiously I approached an
Austrian, who it turned out had smuggled several
people across the border. I asked if he could help me.
I offered him money, not zlotys but dollars and
German marks. In Warsaw I had managed to
acquire some foreign exchange. Imperturbably he
took nearly all my cash, but he took me with him
and that was all that mattered.

'We crossed the Yugoslav border into Austria
without a hitch. The officers of the gendarmerie
there arrested me because I had no passport. I
begged for political asylum and was taken to the
refugee camp in Traiskirchen, not far from Vienna.
Four weeks later I received an alien's pass. On my
first day in the camp I had written again to the registration bureau in Kassel but this time I enclosed an
international receipt coupon. The answer came fast,
and I had Helen's precious address! Nothing could
hold me back now. I received the money for the
ticket to Kassel from the Joint Distribution Commit-

tee, the Jewish aid society.

'I left immediately. I spent the night on the train.
The trip seemed endless. I felt feverish. Shouldn't I
have written to Helen first that I was coming?
Prepared her for the fact that I was alive? I could
only hope that she would somehow be able to bear
the devastating shock of my standing before her so
unexpectedly, a visitor from the beyond . . .

'I left my small suitcase in the baggage room at
the Kassel station. A taxi took me to the address, a
three-storey post-war building in the inner city. As I
got out of the cab, my knees were shaking. I don't
know how I managed to summon the strength to
climb the stairs. Helen's apartment was on the
second floor. At her door I hesitated. I had to calm
down. My heart was pounding crazily. Seconds
passed. To me it seemed minutes until I dared ring
the bell. The door opened. A young man stood
before me. Schulze. From our camp. A phantom.
My nerves were shot up. I closed my eyes, opened
them again – no doubt about it – it was Schulze as I
remembered him, with his blond hair, a little red
gleaming in it, his grey-green eyes, his narrow lips.
Not very tall. He was looking at me expectantly.
And I was choking.

'I stood there petrified, unable to utter a sound.
Was it a nightmare? Was I awake? It was all utterly
incomprehensible! As if through a fog I heard the
young man ask, ''What do you want?'' In the back-
ground I could hear the voice of a woman, a voice I

knew. Of course, in the past that voice had spoken Polish. "Marek, if it's a salesman, tell him we're not buying anything."

'Suddenly I realized that the young man couldn't be Schulze, if only because of his age. He looked about eighteen. It was clear to him that something extraordinary was going on. "Mother!" he cried. "This man isn't selling anything. I don't think he's feeling well. What shall I do? Mother, bring a glass of water!" I heard steps. Suddenly Helen was standing in front of me. She was crying, "Max! Max!" over and over again.'

Max was trembling. I knew that it was almost unbearable for him to recall these most bitter moments of his life, moments of the most profound humiliation. What he was telling me was so immense, so extraordinary, that I too was speechless. I rose and took him to his room, murmuring something to calm him, and told him that we would talk again later. I left the room. I didn't know if Max even heard me. His behaviour yesterday and last night – so that was it! I thought I was beginning to understand, but there were some things he would still have to explain to me.

An hour later I knocked on his door. No answer. I pressed down on the handle. The door was locked. I called him. I knocked louder and called his name again. Still there was no sound inside the room. Had something happened to him? I should go down and fetch someone and have the room opened. Max might need a doctor. While I was wondering what to do, the door opened. He was standing before me, looking as if I had awakened him from a deep sleep.

'Have you been here a long time? I'm sorry. I was fast asleep. I had the feeling that someone was knocking on the door, but I thought I was dreaming. Come in, Simon. I am going to tell you all about my meeting with Helen. You can see that I am in full control of myself again.'

As I sat down, Max paced up and down the room. 'So that was our reunion. Dear God, after all the years of suffering, of hope, fear, and torment, I had expected something different. All I could stammer over and over again was "How good that you are alive! How good!" We were still standing at the threshold of the open door. We could hear the boy's voice from inside the apartment: "Mother, don't you want to come in?"

'Helen led me into a room, which I noticed later was pleasantly furnished. She asked me to sit down. She sat opposite me. Suddenly I was overwhelmed by the utter exhaustion of my twenty-year search for Helen. I felt drained.'

Max continued. 'If it wasn't Schulze who walked into the room now, then who was it? The young man placed three glasses and a carafe with orange juice on the table in front of us. I forced myself to look at him although it hurt excruciatingly. The likeness to Schulze – it could mean only one thing. I didn't dare to follow the thought to its conclusion. There

was a sour taste in my mouth, a rumbling in my
stomach. I was afraid I was going to vomit.
"Mother," he had said, so he had to be Helen's son.
I looked from him to Helen and asked miserably,
"Are you married? I shouldn't have come here like
this. I should at least have let you know, instead of
plunging into your new life without any warning."
She answered quietly, "Marek and I live alone,
much too alone for the boy, yet . . ." She stopped in
the middle of the sentence. Her cheeks were slightly
flushed. I could tell she was finding talking to me
difficult as long as the boy was in the room. He must
have noticed it. He rose, slightly embarrassed, and
left the room.

'Helen began to cry. The tears poured helplessly
down her cheeks. She was still beautiful. Now I
wanted to comfort her, but words failed me. So I
took her hand and held it firmly. A paradoxical
situation. Moments ago everything in me had risen
up against this woman. The boy with Schulze's face
had sufficed as a reproach. But Helen's tears washed
such thoughts away. She looked so helpless, so
infinitely touching. I felt guilty and reproached
myself. How inconsiderate of me to have turned up
so unexpectedly without letting her know. I had
come running to her like a lovesick student to a girl
he hasn't seen for two days! And almost twenty
years separated us. I hadn't wanted to believe it –
now I had to.

'Her son, Marek, was another man's child, the

child of a murderer. A butcher of human beings. What was I doing here? I felt like getting up and leaving without another word. But I couldn't. In spite of everything, I felt drawn to Helen, the sight of her, the expression in her eyes which I knew so well. I stayed. We had to talk.

'Hesitantly I began to tell about my escape, and again I felt guilty. When we decided that I had to escape, I had promised to get her out of the camp. Instead of which . . . I told her that if we had stayed together, we would at least have died together. I reminded her that she had been the one who urged me to flee. All she said was "Max, I remember everything as if it had been yesterday." I admitted I had reproached myself for years on her account, and how hard it had been to live with these thoughts. I told her about my years in Russia, my long, fruitless search for her, the meeting with Wanda, my escape through Yugoslavia. Helen must have felt it was a blessing for me to be able to rid myself of the burden I had carried with me for years. I think I talked for more than two hours before I told her everything. I didn't look at the clock, I looked only at her and tried to read from her expression what she was thinking. She seemed to concentrate totally on what I was saying, but her eyes betrayed her. She had looked at me like that, so tenderly, the last time in the camp, when we said goodbye. It comforted me. I heard her say, "Max, you didn't really leave me. It was the merciless times that separated us."

'I forgot the boy, forgot the circumstances that had brought us together again, all I felt was that with every passing moment I was calming down. Now she at least knew my side of the story. Only a slight noise next door reminded me the boy was there. He would always be there . . .'

Max poured himself some vodka, a full glass. He must have bought another bottle when I wasn't with him. The bottle was more than half empty. I waved away his offer to pour me a drink. 'And now you shall hear what Helen had to tell me.'

The expression on Max's face prepared me for the worst.

'Well, the Ukrainian had kept his promise. It was late in the evening before he got back to Zalesie. When Schulze saw him coming alone, he roared at him and slapped him before the poor man could open his mouth to explain what had happened. But he was so convincing everyone believed his story. Schulze, the prisoners and the other Ukrainians, and just imagine, Simon, even Helen believed he was telling the truth. Actually it was not impossible that the SS had foiled our plan, and what had been such a meticulously thought-out deception became bitter reality. Schulze spent days phoning various offices, naturally without coming up with anything. In the end he gave up. But he vented his wrath on Helen. He knew she was my fiancée, and he had desired her ever since he laid eyes on her. He forced her to take a room in his house. Helen knew at once what this would mean and thought of committing suicide. The only thing that stopped her was her sister, Miriam, who would have died miserably without her. Schulze, master over life and death, exploited Helen shamelessly. He knew he would never have a better weapon to use against her than her frail sister. After he raped Helen, he freed Miriam from all work on the construction site. That was his way of expressing his gratitude! From then on Miriam was allowed to clean the house without supervision. Thus the sisters saw each other daily, and Helen was able to pass on to Miriam some of the superfluous food in Schulze's house.

'Helen told me how again and again she tried to defend herself against Schulze's advances, to no avail. The more she repulsed him, the greater his desire for her seemed. Two months later Helen realized she was pregnant, and she told Schulze. He went raving mad. She said that for a long time he wondered if he ought to shoot her. Four days before the camp was liquidated, he demanded that she give him a picture of herself. She had none besides the one on her identification card. Schulze tore it out and went off with it. Later he gave her a pass with the name of a Polish peasant woman from the village of Kudrynce, near Skalat.

'Two days later, before the SS liquidated Camp Zalesie, Schulze took Helen to Zloczow in a horse cart, and from there by train to Lemberg. She had refused in vain to leave the camp without Miriam.

Schulze beat her brutally into the cart. The sisters were not even permitted to say goodbye. In Lemberg he put her on a train to Krakow. Helen, who scarcely knew what was happening to her, gave in apathetically. In Krakow the station mission found her a place to sleep in a convent. She pretended she was a Polish fugitive from Soviet-occupied Kudrynce and, until the birth of her child, she was a cleaning woman in the convent. The child, Schulze's child, was born in a hospital. In the meantime the Germans had left and the Russians were occupying the city. What was Helen to do? In her despair she confessed to me that she had even thought of killing the child.

'Simon, I wept over what she told me. Until then I had listened to her reluctantly. Sometimes I even wished that Helen had carried out her threat and killed herself or the child. But now I was overwhelmed by a great feeling of compassion. I would have liked to take Helen in my arms and caress her. Yet I couldn't. I thought of how Schulze's hands had touched her body . . .

'Helen was fully aware that her life with the boy would be hell on earth. She was a lost soul. She avoided any contact with Jews because they would have been suspicious. In those days scarcely any Jewish children were born. She had no choice. She remained Polish.

'She left Krakow and moved frequently from place to place, in constant fear of coming across

someone she knew. The meeting with Wanda was
the last straw. Helen decided to leave Poland and go
where nobody could possibly know her, where she
would be a stranger, she and the unwanted child. He
existed and had a right to live.'

I couldn't help admiring the way Max was
behaving. He was trying so hard to control himself.
And not a trace of reproach in what he had to tell.
In no way did he accuse Helen or say anything to the
effect that in the end her sacrifice had been in vain.
Because the life Helen had tried to protect,
Miriam's, was snuffed out with all the rest. Helen
could not save her sister. Max said, 'Her child was
her fate. It prevented her from returning to the
Jewish community. It was the child that forced her
to live among strangers and avoid making friends.
Helen read all the court reports on the prosecution of
Nazi criminals. She hoped and at the same time
feared that the name Werner Schulze might come
up. Were there no plaintiffs because except for her
there were no more witnesses? The thought must
have weighed heavily upon her at the time.'

Max looked at me as if he were hoping for some
sort of confirmation of what he had just said, or at
least a gesture on my part. In a mixture of
embarrassment and stubbornness he burst out, 'So
now you know. Everything else has nothing to do
with Schulze and concerns only Helen and me!'

'Max,' I said, 'that isn't fair. How can I help if
you keep me in the dark about what took place

between Helen and you after that? And there is the boy. I can't come to a decision unless I know it all.'

'You're right, Simon. I can see your point. And you shall hear the rest . . . I asked Helen if Marek knew who his father was. She turned pale and looked at me with a tortured expression. "He must never know who his father was," she implored me. "He would kill himself." She confessed that in order to protect Marek she had woven a legend about his origin. She had told him that his father was a Jew who had been killed at the end of the war while fighting the Nazis, after having escaped from a concentration camp. So far she had managed to conceal his father's name in all his papers. That hadn't been too difficult because there was no one around from those days who could have checked on the truth of her statements. We decided that as far as I was concerned, we would tell the boy the truth. There was no reason why he shouldn't know that we had gone to school together. We should also tell him that we had been in the same camp. Our love on the other hand did not concern him, not to mention that we had once been engaged.

'Later that night we asked the boy to join us. He hadn't gone to bed but was waiting up in his room, curious. He engaged me in a conversation. I was the first Jewish friend of his mother's he had ever seen besides the man she had known before the war. He listened with interest to what I told him about my experiences in the Soviet Union and in Poland. He was frank about everything and very polite. I must say I couldn't help but like him. But when he smiled, the likeness between him and Schulze was strong. I admit that I found this unbearable, and it was the reason I didn't want to spend the night with them, in spite of the lateness of the hour. Marek and Helen didn't want to let me go. They urged me to stay the night. I was dead tired and gave in. I could no longer refuse Marek's offer to let me have his room. What reason could I have given without hurting his feelings? But I couldn't sleep. I spent the night dressed, sitting at a table, and looking at the pictures of Helen and Marek on the wall. The boy had had a few of them enlarged. For me they were pictures of Helen and Schulze. And yet I could sense that mother and son were happy with each other. I could feel it, see it. I brooded. There was no other man in Helen's life, the love of her youth had remained her only love, and that love had been declared dead, or at least lost. Crazy thoughts flashed through my mind. Perhaps she had hoped that I had died and would never come back and tear open the old wounds. She would have remained alone with her oppressive secret, with her son as her only consolation. No, I should not, could not think thoughts like that! How could I, who after all had left her, have the right?

'I stayed in Kassel for three days. I had found Helen only to leave her again. I could not endure the living reminder of Schulze. I did not reproach her. I assured her over and over again that she had had no alternative. Suicide or murdering her child – these could hardly be called choices. I admit, the whole thing was too much for me. I simply could not come to terms with the reality.

'Helen fought a hopeless battle for me. She mentioned that Marek would soon be starting his medical studies in Munich and then wouldn't need her any more. He was strong enough to go his way alone. She had saved enough money and was therefore independent. She didn't care where we lived: here in Kassel with her or in Paris, where I had work and was making a living, if only we could be together! Everything she said made sense and seemed acceptable, but it had no effect on me. For all the years we'd been apart Helen had been the only woman in the world for me. Now that we were together again at last, an invisible wall separated us. Schulze. His child stood between us. He would forever remind me of his detested father. I was not blessed with the gift of forgetfulness. Did Helen, could Helen realize that my revulsion towards the boy was stronger than anything else? That neither iron common sense nor the greatest discipline could help me? In the end I told her she should go on living as if I were dead, as if I were no longer available. For me she would exist as she did in the photograph I had managed to save over the years. I set her free, free forever. Weeping, she let me go. She saw there was no hope of holding me.

'I have poured out my heart to you. Simon. By now you know all my thoughts, and must have grasped why I can't testify. If Schulze is brought to trial, Helen's and Marek's lives would be ruined. The boy would find out who his father really was. Schulze could haul Helen into court as a defence witness. In his perverse mind he could insist that he had saved a Jewish girl's life. That must not happen! Helen has suffered enough. She has the right to be left in peace.'

Max confused me. Too much had poured in on me during these last hours. I couldn't give him a definite answer right away, I had to think this case over carefully. Max misunderstood my silence. He urged me, 'Simon, the dead that Schulze has on his conscience can't be brought back to life by my testimony. But the living, Helen and Marek, could be ruined by it. It's a paradox, but their right to a peaceful life depends on criminals like Schulze being allowed to go on living as free citizens. And don't forget the filth the press would pour over Helen. The dregs of society would delight in her misfortune. You can't want that, Simon, even if the justice you serve is impeded. I personally have nothing against a lawsuit that would bring down Schulze, but for Helen's sake, I beg you not to go through with it!'

Hesitantly I told him, 'It would be the first time I have let a criminal go free against whom I have such clear-cut evidence. But very well, if Schulze is to go free, it must depend on you and Helen only. You two shall decide. You are probably the only survivors of the camp he commanded. Believe me when I say I didn't leave a stone unturned to find other witnesses to his crimes. And failed. I want you to consider carefully – does he really deserve your protection? Don't you owe his prosecution to those who are no longer here? Helen wanted you to survive above all to bear witness. Is this really no longer of any importance to her? Aren't you exaggerating the danger of such a trial for her and Marek? Forgive me, intuitively I feel you are right, but I would like to hear from Helen herself that she does not wish Schulze to be judged for his crimes. You must understand that, Max!'

'So go and see her, Simon. I have nothing against it. I don't know of course if she will be willing to speak about herself to you, a stranger. Spare her as much as you can. Don't make an interrogation of it. I'm sure she will think I sent you to her because I want to hurt her. Must you really open up all the old wounds?'

'Max,' I said, 'you have told me exactly what you wanted to tell me. I forced nothing out of you. Everything you revealed, you did freely. Helen too will tell me only as much as she wants to tell me. But I must insist on talking to her. You feel that the suffering of the witnesses would stand in the way of justice. I know how terrible it is after so many years when someone has to describe how his child, his father, his wife, was murdered before his very eyes. Don't you think I can judge what that means to the

witnesses after all this time to have to face the
murderers, the torturers? Many broke down during
their testimony or suffered a heart attack! Even so,
would it have been right to forgo the trials? Should
the murderers be allowed to profit once more through
their victims? No, Max. Your case, granted, is
different, and I assure you again, without your and
Helen's permission, Schulze will not stand trial . . .'

Max was furious. He shoved a piece of paper
across the table at me on which he had reluctantly
scribbled Helen's address. It was barely legible.

I continued. 'You behave as if I were inhuman,
as if principles mean more to me than human
beings. But why do you think I am here? Not as a
matter of principle but for you as a human being and
a Jew, and for those who are no longer here to
accuse. We are their representatives. That is the
meaning behind our survival. You have given up on
yourself, on life, and vegetate like a wounded animal.
I know I am being harsh, Max, but it's true. I
couldn't live like that. I want to be there for all those
who were innocent and whose blood was shed. Your
parents and brothers and sisters are among them.'

In the evening I accompanied Max to the airport
in a taxi. We embraced in front of the passport
control. He gave the official his passport, at the same
time saying in my direction, 'Please, Simon, don't
forget. You promised to spare Helen.' I watched
him hurry away until he disappeared behind the
opaque glass of the departure lounge.

5

Now I was in a plane too, flying home to Vienna.
Thinking of the case. I had the criminal and one
witness. For a start that should suffice. I could take
Schulze to court on Max's testimony alone. In this
first phase of the trial, Helen's name would not have
to be mentioned. Of course, Schulze would protest
his innocence, like the coward he was. That's what
most of the Nazi criminals did. Or excuse his
behaviour by saying he had to obey orders, or
pretend not to know what it was all about. Would
the testimony of a single witness suffice to get a
verdict? I was not sure. But Werner Schulze's
reputation in society would be damaged; he would
lose his job even if he was the son-in-law of the
company president. He would become a liability; his
wife would ask for a divorce . . .

Perhaps I could find Balke, who also knew a thing
or two about Schulze. That would strengthen the
indictment. But what if Max was right and Schulze
defended himself? He wouldn't hesitate to involve
Helen. All he would actually have to do is recall the
name of the Polish peasant woman whose papers he
gave Helen. Helen was the key. Everything

depended on her. If she could convince me that I had the right to let Schulze go scot-free, then . . .

In Vienna I found a letter from Fred, enclosing a newspaper clipping showing Schulze as a bowling champion. A jolly group of people surrounded him. They were celebrating his financing of a new automatic bowling alley. Fred wrote that Schulze was a member of the 'best society' in Karlsruhe and was highly respected. In the factory there had been a fight, which was triggered by Schulze's violent temper. Something concerning his past had started it. Fred didn't know whether it concerned a wartime or a post-war incident. He intended to find out more and had put a detective on the case.

Fred's letter gave me pause. If Schulze had employed someone he knew from his SS days, someone who didn't have to fear the courts and who knew more about Schulze than was desirable, and if the two had fallen out and the other man had the courage . . . I might have a second witness.

As a precaution I put the Schulze file in my safe in the bank. For the time being, Helen and Max's secret concerned nobody, not even my collaborators. I had promised Max discretion. I had to think of him constantly. I could imagine how he must be torturing himself for having been so open with me. I wanted to reassure him and so wrote him a short letter.

Dear Max, dear Brother,

I know just how you are feeling. Our talk weighs
heavily upon me too. But please don't worry. I promise
you not to come to any decision until I have spoken to
Helen. I embrace you.

Yours, Simon

Fred sent the detective's report. The bold hope of
perhaps finding another witness burst like a soap
bubble. The fight had only been indirectly
connected with Schulze's Nazi past. It happened because *Herr Direktor* Schulze wanted to force two
young employees to cut their long hair. One of the
young men gave him a suitable answer: the
employees' haircuts were no damn concern of the
firm. Schulze had lost all control, according to the
detective's account, threatened to fire the boys, and
screamed, 'I always knew it! We need a new Hitler,
and we won't have law and order until we get one!'
Whereupon the altercation between the young men
and Schulze developed into a fist fight. Somebody
called the police, the incident was reported. Schulze
denied having said, 'We need a new Hitler.' All he
had meant was that during Hitler's time the administration would have had the right to send the young
men to the barber. He took back the threat of firing
them. They had not brought charges.

There was no purpose in putting off my decision
any longer. I wrote to Helen. I chose my words carefully. I mentioned explicitly that Max had not
suggested I visit her. She answered by return mail:

she knew who I was and expected my visit any time. I should only please let her know the day and time of my arrival. I was pleasantly surprised. I had been prepared for evasiveness and a longer correspondence.

Two weeks later I was standing at her door. The young man opened the door, and I too was shocked by his resemblance to Schulze as I knew him from his photographs. But I was prepared for it. The likeness must have struck Max like a blow. I introduced myself. The boy greeted me pleasantly and added, 'I am very happy to meet you personally. We Jews are convinced of the importance of your work.' Out of Schulze's mouth: 'We Jews . . .' Hard to believe. I asked Marek where his mother was; he replied that she would be with me right away. Instinctively I put my hand in the pocket of my jacket where I had the photos of Schulze. Marek must never see them. He offered me refreshment. There was nothing Jewish about him, yet he felt Jewish. His words confirmed it. He told me that he hoped to make Jewish friends in the course of his medical studies in Munich. Here in Kassel there weren't many Jews, and his mother and he had practically no contact with them. He regretted this. In order to shorten the time while waiting for Helen, and since I noticed how open-minded the young man was about Jewish matters, I told him what I had found out about the suffering of the Jews in Kassel.

'Jews were living in this area as early as the fourteenth century,' I told him. 'When the plague was rampant, they were made the scapegoats and were driven out of the city. There was nothing unusual about that in those days. It happened all over Europe. Later other Jews came and settled in Kassel. They were banished during the Thirty Years War. In the eighteenth century the Jews built a synagogue in Kassel. The Nazis set fire to it during the so-called "Crystal Night" in November 1938. Before Hitler came to power, there were two thousand five hundred Jews living in Kassel. There were two synagogues, an old people's home, an orphanage, a teacher's training college, and a Jewish elementary school. All this the Nazis destroyed, and all the Jews were deported. I don't know how many of them survived the concentration camps, all I know is that only fifty Jews returned to Kassel.'

Marek, who was listening intently, asked me how I happened to know so much about local conditions in Kassel. 'I make a point of looking up the history of the Jews in our archives before I visit a German city,' I explained. 'Usually I also visit the Jewish Community Centre and talk to my fellow believers. I don't know whether I'll have time for it on this visit.'

Marek said he regretted this. I felt sorry for him. He was longing to become a part of the Jewish cause. He even offered to help me. 'I owe it to my father who was killed by the Nazis because he fought them. What *could* I do for him and for our people,

Herr Wiesenthal? Give me something to do, at least try me! I'm sure I'd do a good job.'

I was touched by his naïve eagerness. 'Thank you for offering to help. I know you mean it sincerely.'

'Please don't tell my mother about it. When I heard you were going to visit us, I spoke to her about how anxious I was to support you in your work in whatever way I could. But Mother was absolutely against it. She even went so far as to ask me never to bring up the subject again! In the normal course of events, Mother and I have no secrets from each other, but the thought that I might work for you seems to upset her. I don't know why.'

I changed the subject. I mentioned a man called Escherich who lives in Kassel whom I had met during the war when both of us were working on the highway, he as a civil servant, I as a forced labourer. Escherich always behaved decently towards us forced labourers, I told Marek, who seemed to have read the name somewhere, there was a store by that name . . .

Suddenly Helen was standing in the room. We hadn't heard her come in. I recognized in her the woman whose picture Max carried with him constantly. Her face, with no make-up, was still beautiful. I could see little change. A face that couldn't help impressing any man. What surprised and fascinated me was her complexion, so clear, so youthfully fresh. Only the shock of the last weeks was betrayed in her troubled eyes. She greeted me and I couldn't help saying, 'You look so young,

Helen – I may call you Helen, may I not? Nobody would believe that you had a grown-up son.'

'When I look at Marek I realize how quickly time passes.' She was smiling. Then she asked her son to leave us alone. He had no sooner left the room when she asked nervously, 'Please tell me the truth. It really isn't Max who sent you to me?' By her voice I could tell she hoped the opposite was true. My answer would disappoint her. 'No. He didn't send me. He only gave me your address.'

She looked down to hide her chagrin. 'You know, I wait every day for a letter from Max, a sign of life. Although I should know better. Because he told me that I would have to manage without him in the future too. Live as if he were not alive somewhere in Paris but was dead. I don't know how much he has told you. I have written to him several times. He has my telephone number. But apparently he can't manage to jump over his own shadow.'

'Helen, I know all about your past and Max's. I know that both of you are suffering. Perhaps I can help. But first I must beg you to be strong, to be brave. I have something to tell you that will shock and upset you.' And I couldn't hold it back any longer. 'Schulze is alive!'

She swayed, grasping the back of a chair for support, and stared at me, wide-eyed. Her expression betrayed her incredulity. I was angry with myself. Nobody could have come to the point less diplomatically than I had just done.

'What?' she stammered. 'How . . . how do you know?'

'I found out quite by chance.'

What had I done? The situation must have been unbearable for Helen. I could have spared her the shock. A bringer of dreadful tidings. Why hadn't I chosen my words more carefully? I should have taken more time, a lot more time, and prepared her gradually for what I would have to do to her with my news. 'Where does he live?' I heard her say.

'Not far from here.'

'Good. Tell me where I can find him. I'll go to him and I'll kill him! His death is long overdue.'

I could sense that she meant it, even now when she seemed to be in a trance. 'No, Helen!' I implored her. 'You can't do that. I won't let you. He has ruined enough lives, not your son's now too. Helen, think of Marek, of his future. Marek can't help it if Schulze is his father. Even Max tells me he is a good boy and that only one person in the world means anything to him – you. For his sake don't do anything you will regret later.'

There were beads of sweat on her forehead. I had to keep talking, appeal to her instinct as a mother. I wouldn't stop until she had recovered to some extent. What would she say? The shock of the news that Schulze was alive seemed to be waning. Her face showed colour again. She wanted to tell me something, hesitated, tried again. 'Herr Wiesenthal . . .'

'Call me by my first name, Helen. Max does. We even say *du* to each other because what we have to talk about is so intimate, we should put all formality aside.'

'Simon, do you think . . .' She used the *sie* and corrected herself. 'I mean *du*. Forgive me, I'm still terribly confused. But do you think that the beast believes our child has survived? So much argues against it, doesn't it? I could have died, or done something to prevent giving birth to a child I didn't want. That would have been perfectly natural. An abortion, a miscarriage with all its complications in time of war. A murder, a suicide in those days – who would have cared? Everybody was busy saving his own life. The chance that this child, even if it had been born, might survive was nil. Am I right, Simon?'

I nodded. She barely noticed. The spell seemed to be broken. A shock can also have a healing effect. I felt that now Helen needed someone to listen to her, someone who she knew would understand her. And I was there.

'It would have been the easiest thing in the world for Schulze to have deported me with the others,' she began. 'But he didn't, although he hated us Jews more than anything else in the world. But he was mad about me, and with that he took a great risk because he feared being denounced for miscegenation, for which there was a high penalty, as you know. I hoped this would stop him from taking the final step, but no . . . The Ukrainians were already whispering about us, but they didn't dare report the German. And he had no alibi. His SS judges would hardly have accepted the excuse that he had raped me while drunk. But something quite unexpected happened to him: he didn't bellow all over the place any more, the beatings became fewer, he behaved in a more civilized fashion, life for the prisoners was suddenly easier, but for me life was hell. How often I wished I were dead. I can't express in words the way I felt at the time. Spare me, Simon, I beg of you. If it hadn't been for my sister I would have killed myself, believe me. But with Miriam I could talk about it all. She didn't blame me. She knew that I was doing nothing voluntarily, that only death could put an end to his lust. She tried to console me and pointed out the people in the camp who were being spared Schulze's torture only because of me. I was ashamed in front of the women; there were times when I didn't dare look them in the eye, and yet they behaved wonderfully towards me. Not a trace of contempt, only pity. But I felt nothing but loathing for myself and for him.

'I tried desperately to think of a way out. What if I killed him? That was something I could do. But again Miriam talked me out of it. To kill Schulze meant to kill all the others because the SS would avenge the death of their commander in a horrible fashion. For one of them, fifty or a hundred of us would have to die.

'Then came the time of the German retreat. In the

spring of 1944 Schulze listened to the army reports
for hours. He didn't hear anything good. He swore
and raved. He realized that the defeat of Germany
was at hand. The news from the front gave me
renewed courage. A decision was forming inside me.
I had longed to die, now I wanted to live if only to
see our torturers and murderers hanged! I had a goal
again. Nobody can imagine what that meant to me,
Simon, except someone who has gone through it
himself. I was burning for revenge. Schulze must
have noticed that something in me had changed.
Now he beat me almost daily. For me it was a blessing, compared with his caresses!'

Helen was silent. She looked past me, her eyes
fixed on a spot in the light-patterned wallpaper. I
had to get her to continue. That was the only way I
could help her in her distress.

'Helen, I know how hard this is for you. And to
tell it all to a man . . . that must make it even more
difficult . . .'

She interrupted me. 'I am sure you know the story
of my life through Max. Everything I told him is
true. I didn't lie, I didn't make things easier for
myself. But perhaps you are asking, "Why did she
give birth to the child of this criminal?" I often asked
myself the question when the time came. But everything in me rejected the idea of an abortion. It
wasn't the fault of the tiny being growing inside me.
Nobody had asked him to be born. Of course, I
could have put the child in an orphanage, but he was

my child and I was his mother.

'The boy grew, looking more like Schulze every day. I didn't think I could bear it. Would he inherit Schulze's violent temper, his brutality? Were my fears never to end? But this time they were unfounded. The boy is like Schulze only in appearance. And he is a good boy – compassionate, considerate, and loving. I assure you, Simon, I watched him closely when he was little, and later when he went to school. There is nothing of his father in him, nothing! You believe me, don't you?'

'I do, Helen. Max would see it too if he knew the boy better. Unfortunately, I don't know how we can bring that about.'

'I am sure he would. I always was sure. You can't imagine the circumstances under which I brought up this child. Only God knows why He subjected me to such misery. At first I had no milk for the baby because I was half-starved myself. I had to beg for a piece of bread, take on the filthiest work. I couldn't turn to Jews for help because they would have wanted to know all about me. I was afraid of meeting anyone from Zloczow. Do you know what it means when you are relieved to know that your friends and relatives are dead? I wanted to get out of Poland, where everything reminded me of my tragedy and that of all the others.

'To think of Max was torture. I never doubted he was alive. I longed for him but couldn't wish he would find me because I had this child, Schulze's child. When the boy was little I could still hope that in time he would look like me, or my father, but I soon had to bury this hope too, and I was overwhelmed by the fear that I might meet Max again. I lost my faith in God. I couldn't believe that God would treat His people like that!'

Helen was crying, and I could not comfort her. 'I'm sorry, Simon,' she continued. 'But if you knew how many tears I have shed since I saw Max again. Both of us felt instinctively that the other one was alive, but we found each other only to lose each other again right away. It doesn't make sense. I don't want my son to notice anything, so I cry when I'm alone, and at night when I can't sleep. Just the same, Marek knows something is going on. He has sharp eyes. And I tell him I am weeping because of all those people we have lost, and in a certain way that is true. On the other hand, I consider it my duty to teach him that life also consists of forgetting. I urge him not to cling only to the past. I tell him that means some day being able to forgive.

'But he won't hear a word about that. He is firmly convinced the memory of the Nazi crimes must be preserved. Not only that. He insists there should be retribution. The sins of the fathers . . . Well, you know what I mean, Simon. You must have had such thoughts yourself. As for me – I don't know what to think! Our people – Marek means the Jews – must never forget. And why shouldn't he count himself one of them? According to Jewish law, he is a Jew because his mother is Jewish. Anyway, he identifies wholly with Judaism. I don't know whether to be happy about it or not. Sometimes I think it is Schulze's revenge . . .

'I imagine you would like to know why I came to Germany, of all places. It was a case of circumstances. I left Poland in 1948 with the child on an illegal transport of the *Bricha*. I imagine you remember this Zionist escape organization. We reached Germany via Czechoslovakia and Austria. They brought us to the fugitive camp Föhrwald, near Munich. I was asked if I had any relatives in the West, and where I wanted to emigrate. To Palestine? The Jewish state of Israel had just been founded. I didn't want to go there, not with this child. I wanted to go to Canada or the United States. But I didn't have an affidavit. Who would have vouched for me so that I wouldn't become a burden to the state? No one. So for the time being I had to stay in the camp. I translated refugee documents from Russian and Polish into German.

'One day an American soldier turned up at the camp. He was looking for someone who could translate a Polish letter into German for him. I told him I could, whereupon he brought me a lot of letters and documents to translate. What I was doing got around, and I was offered a job as translator at an American military bureau in Ulm. I was only too glad to leave the camp. In Ulm I had to translate not only letters and documents but also newspaper clippings and other reports. I was getting a good salary, and I enjoyed the work. I could pay for a woman to look after Marek. But after the dissolution of the refugee camp, the office where I was working became superfluous.

'But I had made something of a name for myself as a translator. I took some tests and a few courses in Russian. I received an offer from Kassel, and we moved here. Today I am a qualified court translator for Polish and Russian. You see, Simon, financially we are well off. I can afford to let my son study and to pay for his studies myself. Since there is a trade agreement with the East, I am kept very busy. It was my plan to become independent and open a translation bureau of my own. Then Max came, and since then I haven't made any more plans. On that day my life changed radically. I lost all my self-assurance, my peace of mind. I feel . . . I feel as if I have been derailed. When I got your letter I hoped that Max had sent you to me. I saw a turning point . . .'

'Helen, believe me, there is nothing I would like better. I don't think Max is torturing himself on purpose. It's just that he can't get out of his own skin. In his eyes you are innocent, and he doesn't reproach you, believe me. But fate is against you. A child that so strongly resembles Schulze . . . no, he could never bear it!'

I took the photographs of Schulze out of my pocket, although I was sure I was again doing it at the wrong moment. At first I showed her the oldest picture of him I had. 'Is that him?'

She nodded bravely. 'That's what he must have looked like before he came to the camp. The brutal expression around his mouth is missing. That's not the way I remember him. This face doesn't have the scornful contempt yet . . .'

'Could you bear to look at a picture that shows him as he is today? It's from a prospectus of the firm. I had it photographed and enlarged.'

It was already growing dark in the room. Helen took the photo over to the window and looked at it for a long time. 'He seems to be doing all right, doesn't he?'

'He is second in command in the factory, moves in the best society, is married to the daughter of the president, and has three children.'

Helen shrugged, thought for a moment, then asked, 'And what does Max have?'

I persisted. 'Helen, it is up to you now whether Schulze continues to go free, whether he should be permitted to enjoy a life that is built on lies. I can expose him, a man who boasts about his heroic actions during the war. He's very proud of them. Do you want him to go unpunished, shouldn't I bring him to justice? The indictment alone would ruin him socially. And we have more evidence than we need for a conviction. Proof!'

I didn't receive a reply because just then Marek walked in. Our depressed mood must have disappointed him. He could see that his mother had been crying. Neither Helen nor I felt like talking. Helen went to the kitchen and pretended to be busy. 'Herr Wiesenthal,' Marek asked shyly as soon as we were alone, 'why is my mother crying so much lately? Do you have any explanation? It all began after the visit from this man she had known in her school days. I can remember it exactly. I'm surprised that we've never heard from him again. After all, he's known my mother since they were children. I wanted to write to him, but Mother wouldn't give me his address.'

What was I to say? He meant so well. I saved myself with a few words I should have been ashamed of. 'Your mother will have her reasons.'

Marek was too tactful to show his disappointment. Adroitly he changed the subject and began to talk about my work, in which he was sincerely interested. Helen placed a platter with open sandwiches in front of us, looked first at her son, then at me. 'Herr Wiesenthal,' Marek was addressing me, 'I know you don't talk about cases that are not closed, but one thing I would like to know – are you working on a case right now? Have you tracked down the criminal?'

'Our work will never end, young man, as long as there are people alive who were responsible for the death of millions. Hundreds of Nazi criminals are still running around free. Thousands died before they could be brought to justice for their crimes. Others will go unpunished if we can't succeed in finding witnesses and proof. That is why the testimony of every survivor is so terribly important.'

Helen interrupted. 'That's right. Everybody should contribute, but only as much as he feels he can.'

Was that her final answer to the case of Werner Schulze? Did it mean that she was completely unable to help me?

The boy had a date to go to the movies with friends. He quite obviously didn't want to leave, but he also didn't want to disappoint his friends. 'I'm sure you'll give Mother your address,' he said. 'Every now and then one hears of something. If I ever do, I'll write to you. I keep my eyes open.'

He left us, and I was glad that he existed. I said as much to Helen, but she didn't hear me. She was lost in thought, started up suddenly, and said, 'Do you realize what it would mean to him to find out who his father is?'

'I can imagine.'

'Simon, I cannot testify against Schulze in court. It would come out that he is the father of my child. He would even be capable of demanding his right as a father, and he would certainly win any paternity suit. For Marek that would be a death sentence. Is the beast to get another victim, Simon? The papers would make the most of the story. I can see the headlines: SS man saves the life of a Jewess! Or better still: Jewess exposed as SS whore! Who would profit by it? Justice? Would it be justice if Marek's innocent life were destroyed? Could you do that to him with a clear conscience? I can't believe it. No. I can't believe it.'

In the meantime I realized how right she was. Who was I to ruin the life of this decent young man in the name of the dead? I could not break down the arguments of Max and Helen. They were telling the truth. I had nothing to offer them that would outweigh Marek's life. Now I had to show my colours.

'Helen, Werner Schulze has the luck to be the only criminal I ever let go. Don't worry. I promise you I shall not indict him.'

I took Schulze's file out of my attaché case and began to tear up the papers, the photos too. Helen helped me. She saw to it that everything was torn to shreds. Carefully she collected the scraps of paper and put them in a dish, which she carried out of the room. A little while later I heard the toilet flushing. When she came back into the room, she was smiling.

'I burned it all first in a pot, then I flushed down the ashes. I wanted to be quite sure . . .' And I had to smile too.

'Now that the case of Werner Schulze is settled once and for all, Helen, I would like to tell you something a Catholic priest once told me. Perhaps we can find comfort in his words. At the time I must admit they only made me smile. One day he came to my office. He was anxious to meet me and to talk to me about my work. He felt that I was exerting myself in vain in my efforts to bring criminals in front of an earthly judge. The unvarnished truth would never come to light anyway in such law suits. Justice was always put off with lies. "Leave these criminals to the judgement of God" was his advice to me. I replied that for those who did not believe in God and feared only earthly justice, this would be a neat solution. He felt that my answer was mockery and left me churlishly. Who knows, there may be a judge waiting for Schulze in the hereafter. At least we can hope so.'

Helen said she had one more request. I knew what it was and said hurriedly, 'I shall write to Max and tell him that I consider the case closed, and that the chief witness is a wonderful woman.'

Helen embraced me and I kissed her on the forehead. Later she accompanied me to the station. I pushed down the window of the compartment and looked back. Helen was standing there, and she waved to me until I was out of sight.

I wrote Max a detailed letter. I only mentioned Helen's son in passing. But I considered it important to inform him that the young man had offered to help me in my work. I wrote to Helen too and offered her my support should she ever need it. Max's reply was short and to the point. Helen's was exuberant. She confessed how relieved she was that the file on Werner Schulze was no more.

Peter, my assistant, wanted to know what had happened to Schulze's file. A hopeless case, I told him. As a precaution, I removed Schulze's card from our card index and destroyed it.

Epilogue

VIENNA, APRIL 1967

I had met Helen and Max six years earlier; since then I hadn't seen them. For me those years were filled with work, difficult decisions, travel, and people, and new cases. And I wrote a book, *The Murderers Among Us*. I had just come back to Vienna after the publication of this book in the United States. I found a letter from Fred. Werner Schulze was dead! In fog and ice his car had skidded into a truck on the *Autobahn*, near Augsburg. The chauffeur was only slightly injured, but Schulze, sitting on the seat beside him, died immediately. Fred enclosed the obituaries from the family and the firm, both from the local paper.

I made copies of the obituaries and sent them to Helen and Max with no comment. Max answered with only the words, 'Thank you.' Helen wrote that she believed in God and his justice again.

I had business to attend to in Paris and made a date with Max in a small café on the Boulevard St Michel. Three years had gone by since I had informed Max and Helen of Schulze's death. Max and I were going to meet around three o'clock. He was half an hour late. I looked around for him impatiently. Then I saw him, coming out of the Metro hurriedly, his feet dragging. Now he was standing in front of me, and the sight of him shocked me. His face was as grey as his hair; the corners of his mouth drooped, he looked infinitely bitter. I tried to hide my shock behind a friendly, everyday expression. Too late. But he covered up the situation with the laconic words, 'Yes, Simon, we have both grown older and not more beautiful.' That was his greeting.

The waiter brought us two cognacs. Max asked about my work, my health; he wanted to know how my wife was – not a word about Helen. But I made up my mind to talk about her. Bluntly I came to the point.

'Tell me, Max, are you too proud to ask me about Helen? You know that we correspond. It would be logical for your first question to concern her. After all, it's over nine years now since you have heard from each other. You can't tell me that your interest in her is dead. Did you think I'd start to talk about her casually, and you could listen disinterestedly, as if the whole thing didn't concern you?'

Max was obviously annoyed. With the bony fingers of his right hand he drummed nervously on the marble tabletop.

'Whether you want to hear about it or not, Max, I am going to tell you what I think of you and Helen. You are both suffering. Whom does that help? What use is it? What do you want from Helen? Do you want her to cast off her child, this intelligent, alert boy, who is so solicitous, so attentive? Who has nothing in common with Schulze but this damned likeness? Helen still loves you, you know that, and you still love her. So why . . . why?'

Max wanted to stop me. He beckoned to one of the students selling newspapers of whom there are so many in this district, and bought a paper, some Trotskyist or Maoist or anarchistic rag. But I would not let him off so easily.

'Just a minute, Max! I'm not finished. I've done a lot of thinking about you two. I simply can't settle for the fact that you and Helen can't seem to find your way back to one another. There *must* be a way that is acceptable to both of you!'

'Are you finished? May I say something?'

'Please do.'

'I curse the day I was born and the day I saw Helen again. You are right, the fact that we are still separated makes no sense. But what can common sense do where feelings are concerned? This boy will always stand between us. I could never live with

him. If I were forced to look at him, I would feel
sick! That's the way it is, and it is never going to
change. Why should I raise Helen's hopes when I
know I can't fulfil.them? You know what she means
to me, but to lie, to feign something I don't feel – I
can't do that, for her sake as well as mine. You
know, my father used to speak often of the "miracle
rabbis" to whom people went when they didn't
know what to do. But those people had faith and
could therefore obey the advice the rabbi gave them.
I have no faith any more, Simon, and you are not a
miracle rabbi who knows the answers to everything.'

VIENNA, SEPTEMBER 1971

A year after this meeting I received a card from Max
for the first time, greetings for the Jewish New Year.
A good sign? Helen, from whom I received a New
Year's card every year, and who always wrote a few
lines about what she was doing, had not mentioned
Max for a long time.

MUNICH, JUNE 1973

I came to Munich and was working for a few days at

the Institute for Current Events. I was also visiting a friend who invited me to the graduation ceremony of his son, who had just finished his medical studies. The young man was about the same age as Marek. I asked my friend if his son had a colleague named Marek. Thus I found out that Marek was also graduating. I was happy for mother and son, and looked forward to seeing Helen, whom I would now meet again in such happy circumstances.

Next morning I looked in vain for Marek among the candidates in the auditorium of the university. I couldn't find him anywhere, but Helen, whom I had already met in the entrance hall, laughed and helped me. 'Do you see the young man with the beard? Third from the right, with the long, red-blond hair? That's Marek. That's the way the young people run around nowadays, Simon. It's the fashion. I'm probably the only mother in Germany who is happy that her son looks like that, and you will understand why.'

I understood very well.

'Do you see that girl, almost in the middle, the one in the blue dress?'

'Yes. Who is she?'

'My future daughter-in-law. A Jewish girl from Canada. We're all going to Toronto for the wedding.'

'Congratulations. Will you stay in Canada?'

'No. I'm coming back.'

'By the way, I met Max a few years ago in Paris.'

'I know. He called me up the following day. Thank you, Simon.'

'And?'

'Nothing. His attitude remains the same.'

There! Marek had discovered me. He whispered to his colleagues standing beside him. They all turned to look at me. I waved to Marek.

The festivities were over. I congratulated my friend's son and joined Helen again. 'Herr Wiesenthal, what a surprise! Mother didn't tell me you were coming,' Marek said. The Canadian girl was standing beside him. Her greeting was friendly too.

'Marek talks so often about you. I am so happy to meet you. We in Canada know all about you and what you are doing. As a student I heard you lecture in Toronto.' I looked at Helen. She was proud of both of them, and she had every reason to be. 'Please come and dine with us,' Marek said impulsively.

He took his mother's arm, and his girl's, and ushered them through the crowd. I followed them. Marek had chosen a restaurant nearby. I heard them making plans. The young people intended to remain in Canada. Helen would come back after the wedding. Before I left, I said to her softly, 'When you get back from Toronto, write to him. Not much. Just, "Max, I am alone now." '